Naseby 1645

The triumph of the New Model Army

Campaign • 185

Naseby 1645

The triumph of the New Model Army

Martin Marix Evans • Illustrated by Graham Turner

First published in Great Britain in 2007 by Osprey Publishing,
Midland House, West Way, Botley, Oxford OX2 0PH, UK
443 Park Avenue South, New York, NY 10016, USA
E-mail: info@ospreypublishing.com

A CIP catalogue record for this book is available from the British Library

ISBN: 978 1 84603 078 9

Martin Marix Evans has asserted his right under the Copyright, Designs and
Patents Act, 1988, to be identified as the author of this work.

Page layout by The Black Spot
Typeset in Helvetica and ITC New Baskerville
Index by Alan Thatcher
Maps by The Map Studio
3D bird's-eye views by 3D Origin
Originated by United Graphics Pte Ltd, Singapore
Printed and bound in China through Worldprint Ltd

07 08 09 10 11   10 9 8 7 6 5 4 3 2 1

For a catalogue of all books published by Osprey Military and
Aviation please contact:

NORTH AMERICA
Osprey Direct, c/o Random House Distribution Center, 400 Hahn Road,
Westminster, MD 21157
E-mail: info@ospreydirect.com

ALL OTHER REGIONS
Osprey Direct UK, P.O. Box 140 Wellingborough, Northants, NN8 2FA, UK
E-mail: info@ospreydirect.co.uk

www.ospreypublishing.com

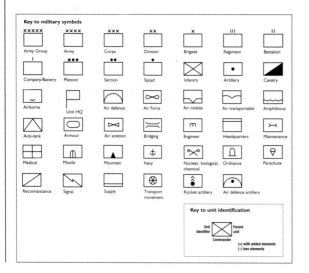

Dedication

For Gillian.
In gratitude for her love, patience and sound good sense.

Artist's note

Readers may care to note that the original paintings from which the colour
plates in this book were prepared are available for private sale. All reproduction
copyright whatsoever is retained by the Publishers. All enquiries should be
addressed to:

Graham Turner, PO Box 568, Aylesbury, Buckinghamshire, HP17 8ZK, UK

The Publishers regret that they can enter into no correspondence upon this matter.

Editor's note

The quotations from the *Diary* of Sir Henry Slingsby contain a number of
common 17th-century abbreviations.
These include:

wch	which	*ye*	the
whre	where	*ym*	them
wn	when	*yt*	that
wth	with		

Acknowledgements

The chief published reference for any modern account of Naseby is the book
by Glenn Foard which appeared only a decade ago. He, like me, was the
recipient of information and guidance from the principal researchers of the
battlefield, Michael Westaway and Peter Burton, who were born and brought
up there and are therefore intimately acquainted with the terrain, and who have
spent literally years in patient, disciplined metal detecting. What is even more
important, they have taken equal care in recording and mapping their work, to
which they are adding even now. My greatest debt of gratitude is to these two
men and their interpretation of their findings.

The farmers to whom the land belongs all deserve thanks for their kindness to
me in permitting entry to their private property, notably Mr David Ball, Mr Albert
Boulton, Mr Cyril Boulton, Mr John Boulton, Mr Roger Chamberlain, Miss Anne
Haddon, Mr and Mrs Ronald Hankins, Mr Jasper Hart, Mr Jim Kelly, Mr
Malcolm Shepherd, Mr and Mrs Richard Tarry and Mr and Mrs William Tarry.

For their generosity in sharing their learning and their views on the English Civil
War, on the way it was fought and on this particular battle. I also thank Nigel
Carren (armourer: www.nigelcarren.com), Stephen Ede-Borrett, Glenn Foard,
Keith Roberts, Christopher L. Scott, Charles Singleton, John Tincey and Malcolm
Wanklyn, in particular, and innumerable members of the Battlefields Trust, the
Sealed Knot, the English Civil War Society and countless patient people who
have been companions on tours of the battlefield. Many of them asked questions
not only to which I lacked answers, but which opened fresh lines of enquiry I had
not thought of. The Northampton Gun Company helped with information on
modern weapons.

The influence of the terrain on the Parliamentarian front and the contribution of
Okey's Dragoons to the start of the fight are ideas I have formed over a number
of years, as are my suggestions of the locations of the incident of Charles's
being prevented from joining the action and of the site of the Parliamentarian
artillery train.

Some of the illustrations and modern photographs come from my own
collection, while others have been included by kind permission of: John Kliene;
Michael Westaway; Paul Woodfield; The Bodleian Library, University of Oxford;
the Syndics of Cambridge University Library; the James Marshall and
Marie-Louise Osborn Collection, the Beinecke Rare Book and Manuscript
Library, Yale University; the Naseby Battlefield Project, the Northamptonshire
Record Office; the Suffolk Record Office and Perry Miniatures (www.perry-
miniatures.com).

The account of events I give here would have been impossible to create
without the contributions of the people I mention above, but the result, full of
doubts and queries, is my responsibility alone. I have tried to adopt as maxims
the words of two men who lived through these events: Oliver Cromwell, *I
beseech you, in the bowels of Christ, think it possible you may be mistaken*,
and Sir Richard Bulstrode *...it is certain, that, in a battle, the next Man can
hardly make a true Relation of the Actions of him that is next him ...So that no
Man give a clear Account ... -.*

Martin Marix Evans
Blakesley, May 2006.

CONTENTS

ORIGINS OF THE CAMPAIGN 7

The military situation • Logistical constraints
The centres of power • Movement • The campaign of 1645

CHRONOLOGY 15

OPPOSING COMMANDERS 17

Royalist commanders • Parliamentarian commanders

OPPOSING ARMIES 22

Equipment, formations and tactics • The New Model Army
The Royalist 'Oxford' Army • Orders of battle

OPPOSING PLANS 36

Parliamentary plans • Royalist plans

THE CAMPAIGN 38

Parliamentary preliminaries • The Royalists' opening moves
The Committee of Both Kingdoms responds
The question of Oxford • The taking of Leicester
The question of Oxford – again • Parliament responds: 2–13 June
The Royalists' week: 7–13 June

THE BATTLE OF NASEBY 54

Battle plans and the start of the day • The New Model advances
The move to Dust Hill • The ground and the battalia • The battle begins
The turn of the tide • The fighting retreat • The final phase

AFTERMATH 86

Hindsight • The fortunes of the king

THE BATTLEFIELD TODAY 91

BIBLIOGRAPHY 94

INDEX 95

Sir Thomas Fairfax from Joshua Sprigge's *Anglia Rediviva* (Naseby Battlefield Project)

On the Cause:

For really I think that the poorest he that is in England hath a life to live, as the greatest he; and therefore truly, sir, I think it's clear, that every man that is to live under a government ought first by his own consent to put himself under that government; and I do think that the poorest man in England is not at all bound in a strict sense to that government that he hath not had a voice to put himself under.

Thomas Rainsborough (or Rainborowe), of the Massachusetts Rainsborough family and Colonel, New Model Army, at the Putney Debates, 28 October 1647.

Kings are justly called gods for that they exercise a manner or resemblance of divine power on earth... God hath power to create or destroy; make or unmake at his pleasure; to give life or to send death; to judge all and to be judged nor accountable to none; to raise low things and to make high things low at his pleasure. And the like power have kings.

James I in a speech to Parliament, 21 March 1610.

ORIGINS OF THE CAMPAIGN

THE MILITARY SITUATION

In January 1642 Charles I had abandoned London after it fell into Parliamentarian hands, and in October the two sides finally met in battle at Edgehill in Warwickshire. The outcome was not decisive, but the opportunity existed for the king to reach London before his enemies and reclaim it for the Royalists; it was squandered and the Royalist army was forced to winter in Oxford. Next spring they secured the West Country, seized control of the North and captured Bristol, but after being forced to abandon the siege of Gloucester Charles was defeated at Newbury on 20 September 1643 and balance was restored. In 1644 events in Scotland and Ireland came into play, with the Scots choosing to support Parliament and a peace of sorts in Ireland releasing forces to reinforce the Royalists.

At the end of June 1644 Charles I had the better of Sir William Waller's army at Cropredy Bridge, near Banbury, and the Royalists managed to evade the attempted pursuit. From Towcester the despondent Waller had written of Parliament's armies to the Committee of Both Kingdoms, which had overall command, saying:

My Lords, I write these particulars [of disaffection and desertion] to let you know an army compounded of these men will never go through with their service, and till you have an army merely your own that you may command it is in a manner impossible to do anything of importance.

In the North the Scots reinforced the Parliamentarian army, which defeated the king's forces at Marston Moor on 2 July, ending the Royalist control of the North, but Waller's view of affairs was reinforced by the failure to defeat and capture the king at the second battle of Newbury in October, to the discredit of the earl of Manchester; this event followed hard on the earl of Essex's defeat at Lostwithiel. The outcome was the creation of the New Model Army, and the events of 1645 would depend massively on the speed with which general officers could be replaced and newly formed units could become operationally effective.

Despite the satisfaction in Royalist circles at the escape from Newbury and the victory at Lostwithiel, the loss of the north of England was a serious setback. The hope of regaining the region, and the supplies and manpower that went with it, was slight given the continuing presence of the Scots army there. The queen was on the Continent attempting to raise reinforcements and supplies which would have to run the gauntlet of Parliament's navy. Further, the hope of raising men from South Wales had been frustrated by defeat at Montgomery. Sir William Brereton wrote the next day, 18 September 1644:

...the Lord so guided and encouraged our men, that with a fresh valiant charge we routed and put to retreat and flight their whole army ... slew (I do believe) 500, wounded many more, took 1,500 prisoners... The enemy's army was reported (and I do believe it) no less than 4,000 – the foot being the old Irish, who came out of Ireland with Col. Broughton, Warren, Tillier...

Monmouth was taken a week later, but the Royalists retook it in November.

The Royalist army was quartered mainly west of Oxford that winter and no restructuring was undertaken other than a shift in commands. Prince Rupert became Lord General and his brother Maurice assumed command in Wales and the Marches. A number of minor actions were attempted, against Abingdon and against Weymouth; neither succeeded in changing the overall position. Parliament took the initiative when Sir William Brereton invested the important town of Chester and Maurice was ordered to relieve the place. To do so he took the remnants of the Irish regiments so badly cut up at Monmouth, now brigaded together as the 'Shrewsbury Foot', from that town, leaving it defended by a couple of hundred men. Brereton withdrew and Maurice entered Chester on 20 February, but Parliamentarian forces seized Shrewsbury in his absence and with it the supplies he had so painstakingly built up there. Moreover, the lines of communication in the West were now compromised.

LOGISTICAL CONSTRAINTS

The decisions taken by both sides in 1645 owed a great deal to the necessities of supporting their war machines. The South-East of England and East Anglia were controlled by Parliament. This gave them the major ports and centres of commerce and agriculture as well as, because of their possession of the navy, the control of much of the import and export business. Even more vital was the possession of the magazines of

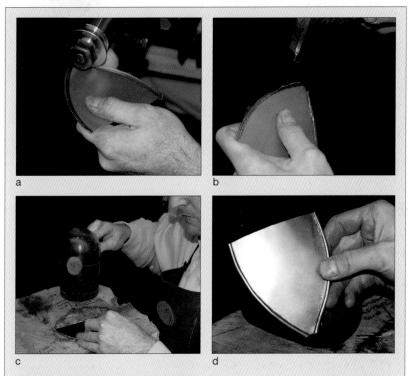

ROLLING THE EDGE OF A CHEEK PIECE
A plate of cold-rolled mild steel, $\frac{1}{25}$in thick, has been cut to shape and (a) **Nigel Carren cranks it through rolling wheels before** (b) **hammering it to close the roll. The piece is then** (c) **curved to a dished shape. The edge of the steel is thus** (d) **suited to being worn close to the skin of the face without cutting the wearer, and is also strengthened against splitting under the impact of an enemy weapon – a characteristic that was increased by incorporating a length of wire within the rolled edge. The raised edge also reduces the likelihood of an enemy blade glancing off the cheek piece into the neck or face. In a manufactory workers would be put to a specific task, literally cranking out the various constituent parts of a helmet. (John Kliene)**

the Tower of London, the Arsenal at Woolwich and the stores at Greenwich and, outside the South-East, the military supplies at Hull and Portsmouth. To these resources was added the output of the arms manufactories in the South-East. Further, the making of gunpowder called for saltpetre (potassium nitrate), of which supplies in England were limited, and for sulphur, which had to be imported from abroad.

Also brought in from overseas were horses and armaments, so that control of the seaports was vital for bare survival, let alone victory. Parliament had not only London, but also King's Lynn, Hull and the south coast ports. This, combined with the loyalty of the navy, eased not only the challenge of obtaining materials, but also that of supplying forces elsewhere with men and arms.

The formation of the New Model Army early in 1645 brought with it a new system of procurement and supply for Parliamentarian troops. A central magazine was established at Reading and two new committees were set up to deal with procurement and distribution. The efficiency of this system contributed substantially to the creation of the New Model Army as an effective fighting force.

Charles I had his court and headquarters in Oxford and his lines of external supply depended on holding the port of Bristol in the South-West and Chester in the North-West to maintain contact with France and with Ireland. In Oxford new industry grew to meet the Royalist demand. As the war continued, Bristol, which had been taken in July 1643, became a major supplier to the Royalist armies, bringing in raw materials both from overseas and from Wales and the Forest of Dean. By February 1644 the Bristol gunsmiths were turning out 200 muskets and bandoliers a week. More industry grew in the West Midlands at Stourbridge and Dudley, sending its output to Oxford by boat down the Severn to Worcester and then overland by cart.

The importance of Ireland as an entrepôt for Royalist arms imports increased the reliance on the ports of the South-West in the supply chain of Charles's armies. The Irish confederates sent agents to Holland, Rome and the leading Catholic courts to acquire arms, while the Parliamentarians traded heavily through the east coast ports, mainly with Holland. Both sides were sensitive in the extreme to even a remote threat to these lines of supply. Carriage of supplies was conducted both by water and on land. Parliament used King's Lynn and London as distribution centres, moving goods to the magazine at Cambridge by the rivers Ouse and Cam and to the stores in Reading by way of the Thames. The supply of outposts such as Gloucester posed considerable problems. Convoys of wagons or pack-horses had to be protected by armed escorts drawn from the army. The Royalists' difficulties were even greater. The Thames served to move arms from Oxford to Abingdon and Wallingford, but most of the shipments were by road and were therefore vulnerable.

It was also necessary to provide troops with food and drink. As long as funds could be raised by various forms of taxation, payment for the basic requirements of bread, cheese and beer for the men and hay, oats and pulses for the horses could be made. Such payment was at times in the form of vouchers to be redeemed subsequently, and those of the Royalists, who were forced to increase their voucher use as the war continued and their taxable territory decreased, ultimately were not reimbursed. While an infantryman carried about one week's food supply in his snapsack, meat was obtained locally by purchase or plunder. The movement of troops around the country was accompanied by loss to the local population, somtimes compensated for, but loss all the same. This contributed to the emergence of irregular forces, armed with whatever they could lay their hands on, with a non-partisan animosity to each and every fighting force. The Clubmen, as they were known, were an additional source of annoyance to troops on the march.

THE CENTRES OF POWER

The Parliamentarian East of England was protected by garrisons north of London holding Aylesbury, Newport Pagnell, Northampton, and, on the course of the River Welland, Rockingham, near Kettering, and Crowland, south of Spalding. From these secure bases convoys could strike out westwards to supply such crucial barbs in such Royalist communication lines as Gloucester, which was reached by way of Coventry and Warwick. A line of strongpoints ran north-west through Leicester and Derby, but it passed through a gap between two Royalist areas of influence based at Belvoir Castle, west of Parliamentarian Grantham, and Ashby de la Zouch, north-west of Leicester.

The Royalist capital of Oxford was surrounded by a scatter of garrisons, with a line running north towards Banbury, where the country became Parliamentarian until the Ashby–Belvoir gap. From Belvoir the way lay clear to Newark, which had been in Royalist hands since 1642. This was the route to the North. To the west Charles's influence was based on Bristol and Chester along the Welsh Marches, with the exception of Gloucester.

The country in between the garrisoned centres was at all times uncertain, liable to unexpected incursions and disputed by rival patrols. In 1643 the territory east of the Banbury–Oxford line was invaded by the Royalists. On 15 October Prince Rupert led 22 troops of horse and 700 foot from Oxford against Northampton, where it was hoped their sympathizers would help them enter the north of the town. Major Nathaniel Whetham, the governor of the place, had his scouts in the field and the approach of the enemy was detected early, according to *The True Informer* of 21–28 October 1643. He sent out a party of 24 horse, which had a brisk skirmish with Rupert's scouts at Brampton Bridge (near Chapel Brampton), 3 miles north of the town, killing one of them. The patrol returned to Northampton by the North Gate as ordered, where Whetham had taken position in the gate-tower and lined the walls with musketeers. The moon was bright enough to reveal his returning horse who were shouting for admittance, with Royalists in hot pursuit. A volley of musket fire made the pursuers pause enough for the gate to be opened, let the patrol back in, and slam it in the faces of the Cavaliers. Surprise lost, Rupert brought his infantry up and formed them near St Andrew's Mills, whence they were driven off.

The Royalist attempt to make Newport Pagnell an outpost of their own was frustrated by the approach of Sergeant-Major-General Philip Skippon's force. The Parliamentarians secured the abandoned town on 28 October, and with it the crossing of the London to Northampton route with the Bedford to Oxford road. The Royalists occupied Towcester, on Watling Street, instead, and thus the route from London to Daventry and Coventry. In the end there was no need to storm Towcester, for Rupert pulled his forces out on 21 January 1644 in order to mount an assault on Aylesbury.

Farther north, Leicester remained almost untroubled in the early years of the war. In June 1642, after a bloodless confrontation, the town passed into Parliamentary hands. The king raised his standard at Nottingham and Leicester was threatened when Rupert demanded

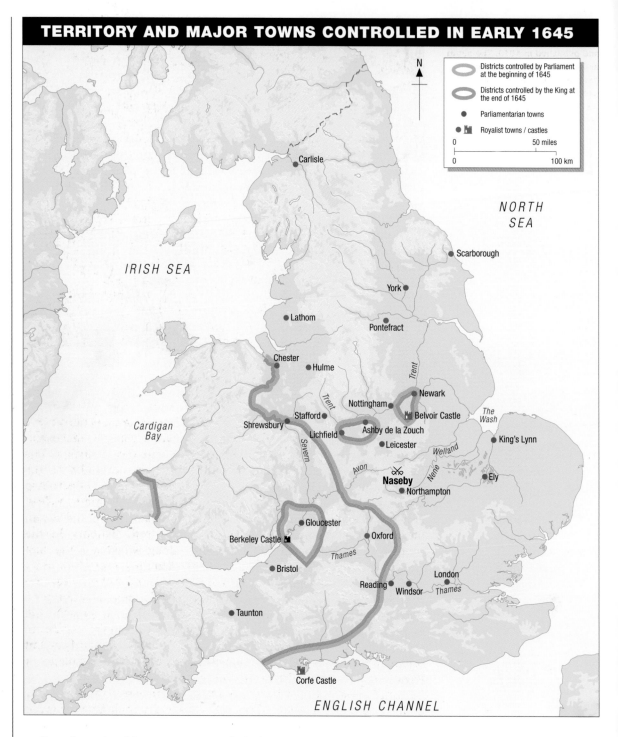

N

Districts controlled by Parliament at the beginning of 1645

Districts controlled by the King at the end of 1645

● Parliamentarian towns

● Royalist towns / castles

| 0 | 50 miles |
| 0 | 100 km |

NORTH SEA

Carlisle

IRISH SEA

Scarborough

York

Lathom

Pontefract

Chester

Hulme

Trent

Stafford

Nottingham

Newark

Belvoir Castle

Cardigan Bay

Shrewsbury

Lichfield

Ashby de la Zouch

Leicester

The Wash

King's Lynn

Severn

Welland

Nene

Ely

Avon

Naseby

Northampton

Gloucester

Berkeley Castle

Oxford

Thames

Bristol

Reading

London

Windsor

Thames

Taunton

Corfe Castle

ENGLISH CHANNEL

a fine, but the king countermanded the imposition and Royalist attentions turned elsewhere.

The country from Newport Pagnell in the south to Leicester in the north became well known to both sides between 1642 and 1645. It was frontier territory, perhaps with a populace inclined rather more to one side than the other, but often apparently friends to whoever rode up armed and demanding food and fodder.

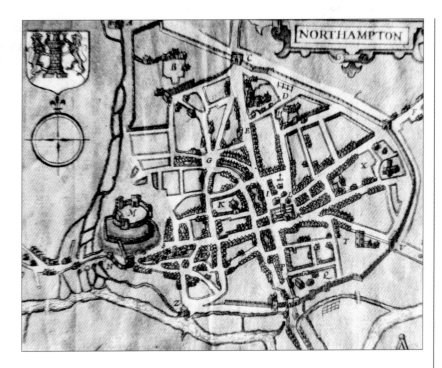

The map of Northampton 'performed' by John Speed and published in 1610. The south and west of the town enjoyed the protection of rivers and walls, while the condition of the rest of the defences gave cause for concern.

MOVEMENT

Although they may have had experience of the country, commanders, and especially quartermasters, had to be able to plan the movement of large bodies of men for the conduct of a serious campaign. The country between Northampton and Leicester, known today as the Northamptonshire Uplands, appears to modern eyes as a gentle, rolling landscape with numerous little streams at the foot of modest valleys. However, if explored on foot or horseback, the challenges of the terrain become clear. A discontinuous ridge runs from Banbury in the south-west to Naseby in the north-east, along which a route past Cropredy Bridge to Daventry runs as far as Watling Street. Even today road, rail and canal squeeze through a saddle at Watford Gap and streams east of Watling Street constrain roads from Northampton towards Rugby, Leicester and Market Harborough to ridges. On the maps of the day, derived from those created by Christopher Saxton in the previous century, roads did not appear, nor did hills and valleys. But bridges were shown and the rivers were marked, as well as the names of towns, together with indications of their size.

Large bodies of men moved as a number of lesser bodies, making their way to a predetermined rendezvous. Cavalry could go very much where it pleased, and foot soldiers might, given favourable weather, make their way over fields and streams. Wheeled transport, the baggage and artillery trains, was more tightly constrained and the positions of bridges on the map and by report or local knowledge were useful information to have. The summer of 1645 was unusually wet and thus the route taken by an army would be influenced significantly by roads and bridges, and, regardless of weather, by appropriate landmarks to serve as navigational aids: windmills and church towers as a rule.

Detail showing the cherubs decorating the title page of John Ogilby's *Britannia* (1675), which brandish examples of contemporary mapping. On the left a route description, in the centre a city map and on the right an innovation made since the war, a map with roads.

THE CAMPAIGN OF 1645

The Royalist campaign started with a vigorous effort to restore control of the Marches, with Lord Astley, Charles Gerard from South Wales, Sir Marmaduke Langdale with his Northern Horse and princes Rupert and Maurice in the field with some 8,000 men. The position of Chester was secured for the time being, and the Royalists turned south to deal with the Clubmen. Other forays were undertaken. Lord Goring swept through Hampshire to little purpose and then withdrew to Salisbury at the end of January. In late February and early March Langdale led an expedition of horse to the relief of Pontefract, which he achieved for a brief space, in which it was resupplied. He was back in Newark on 4 March. It had been a remarkable exercise, but was a part of a series of disconnected actions without strategic coherence.

Action in response to Parliamentarian threats continued. Waller and Cromwell were ordered to go to the relief of Taunton. Goring responded, but disagreements with the king's Devon and Cornwall forces frustrated his intention to bring the enemy to battle in March and the summons to return to form the New Model Army took them back to Berkshire with little achieved on either side. All this activity had left Parliament the leisure to re-form its army and impress new recruits with minimal disturbance while Royalist recruitment other than in the South-West had been modest. Meanwhile the principal Royalist force remained in Oxford. The lack of strategic vision that would lead to Royalist defeat was already evident.

CHRONOLOGY

1644

2 July	Royalist army under Prince Rupert defeated at Marston Moor.
16 July	Surrender of York to the Parliamentarians.
1 September	Essex leaves his army at Lostwithiel and it surrenders to Charles I the next day; Montrose wins for Charles I at Tippermuir.
13 September	Montrose victorious at Aberdeen.
20 October	Scots capture Newcastle.
27 October	Second battle of Newbury; Royalists succeed in withdrawing after dark.
19 December	Self-Denying Ordinance passed by the House of Commons.

1645

10 January	Archbishop Laud executed.
11 January	The New Model Ordinance approved by the House of Commons.
21 January	Fairfax appointed to command the New Model Army.
19 February	Prince Maurice leaves Shrewsbury to relieve Chester.
21 February	Royalists lose Shrewsbury to Sir Thomas Mytton.
1 March	Langdale relieves Pontefract.
3 April	House of Lords passes the Self-Denying Ordinance.
22 April	Prince Rupert, from Bristol, defeats Massey at Ledbury.
24 April	Cromwell attacks Royalists at Islip.
30 April	New Model Army marches from Windsor to Reading.
7 May	New Model Army at Blandford, Dorset; Charles I and the Oxford Army leave Oxford, northwards.
9 May	Royalists in Taunton town, but castle holds; Fairfax sends three regiments of foot and one of horse to Taunton; New Model Army heads back to Ringwood, Hampshire.
11 May	Royalists withdraw from Taunton town; New Model Army at Romsey, Hampshire; Royalists at Droitwich.
17 May	Fairfax ordered to invest Oxford; Vermuyden ordered to support the Scots in the North.
20 May	Charles at Market Drayton; Brereton abandons siege of Chester.
22 May	New Model Army at Marston; siege of Oxford begins.
26 May	Vermuyden recalled, Cromwell ordered to Ely.
29 May	Royalists to Leicester.
31 May	Leicester stormed and taken by Royalists.
5 June	Royalists to Market Harborough and their horse outside Northampton.
6 June	New Model Army to Great Brickhill, Buckinghamshire.
7 June	Royalists to Daventry.
9 June	New Model to Stony Stratford, Buckinghamshire.
10 June	Cromwell appointed Lieutenant-General; Fairfax's trumpeter on embassy to Royalists on Borough Hill.
11 June	Skirmishes in Towcester area; New Model to Wooton, near Northampton.
12 June	New Model to Kislingbury, near Northampton; Royalists to Market Harborough.
13 June	Fairfax, in early hours, sees Royalist shelters burning on Borough Hill; New Model to Guilsborough; patrols clash at Naseby.
14 June	Battle of Naseby.
18 June	Leicester retaken by Parliamentarians.
2 July	Montrose wins at Alford.
10 July	New Model Army defeats Goring at Langport.

15 August	Montrose wins battle of Kilsyth.
10 September	Prince Rupert surrenders Bristol.
13 September	Montrose defeated at Philiphaugh.
24 September	Langdale defeated at Rowton Heath.
14 October	Parliamentarians storm Basing House.

1646

16 February	Royalists defeated at Torrington.
21 March	Last Royalist field army, Astley's, defeated at Stow-on-the-Wold.
5 May	Charles I surrenders to the Scots.
20 May	Oxford surrendered by the Royalists.

OPPOSING COMMANDERS

ROYALIST COMMANDERS

King Charles I (1600–49) commanded the Royalist forces in spite of his lack of practical experience. However, by 1645 he had seen two years of the war in England and had benefited from advice from officers with experience of the Thirty Years War on the Continent. His achievements included the highly successful campaign against the earl of Essex's army at Lostwithiel in the late summer of 1644. Based in Oxford, his ability to control his armies was limited by distance and the lack of clarity in the chain of command. He had a tendency to act on the advice of the person most recently consulted and his views were shaped in an intense correspondence with his wife, Henrietta Maria, the daughter of Henry IV of France.

Portrait of Charles I painted by Anthony van Dyke in 1635. (Copyright Akg-images)

Prince Rupert, Count Palatine of the Rhine and Duke of Bavaria (1619–82) has been portrayed as a cavalry commander of flair and courage, flawed by impetuosity and romantic glory-seeking. Although only 22 years of age, he was already an experienced officer before he came to England and he led his troops to many notable successes. Rupert served in the imperial cavalry in the Thirty Years War and his experience, including the siege of Breda in 1637, gave him an understanding of artillery, fortifications and siege-craft. As soon as the Civil War began he joined his uncle's army. His first advice was to fortify loyal towns and use cavalry to harry the Parliamentarian besiegers; it was not taken.

In 1644 Rupert began with successes but he was defeated at Marston Moor on 2 July. By 1645 Rupert's relationships with Charles's other advisers were dangerously poor. In September, after Naseby, Rupert was forced to yield Bristol to Fairfax, an act Charles regarded as near-treachery. It brought their relationship to an end.

George, Lord Digby (1612–77) was a member of Charles's court and of his council of war, although he had no previous military experience. He fought at Edgehill and allowed his men to take part in the pursuit of the enemy cavalry, claiming that he was unaware of his role as reserve. In spite of this error he was made a secretary of state. He had a deep animosity towards Prince Rupert.

Sir Edward Walker (1612–77) was Secretary at War to Charles from 1642 and to the Privy Council from 1644, and was to serve Charles II in the same capacity in exile. He was critical of Prince Rupert both during the war and in his memoirs, *Historical Discourses upon Several Occasions*. This was written in about 1647, but not published until 1705. Walker's works influenced the history of the war as written by Edward Hyde.

Sir Edward Hyde (later Earl of Clarendon) (1609–74) was an adviser to Charles and in January 1645 he took part in the unsuccessful peace negotiations at Uxbridge. In March he accompanied the Prince of Wales into the West Country and was thus absent from Naseby. The 1645 part of his *History of the Great Rebellion* was written between 1671 and his death, and relies heavily on Edward Walker's work on the Naseby campaign.

Lord (formerly Sir Jacob) Astley (1579–1651) was Sergeant-Major-General of Foot to Charles. He had served in the Dutch army from the age of 18 and was military tutor to Prince Rupert. He was created baron in November 1644 and fought on after Naseby, surrendering the last Royalist field army at Stow-on-the-Wold in 1646.

George Lisle (d. 1648) served in the Low Countries before joining the Royalists. He fought at the first battle of Newbury, at Cheriton and, with notable valour, at the second battle of Newbury. He was executed after the siege of Colchester at the orders of Fairfax.

Prince Maurice (1620–52) was Rupert's younger brother and served in Holland with him from 1637. With his brother he joined the Royalist army in August 1642, led his own regiment at Edgehill and then fought in various theatres in England with no small success. He was lost at sea in September 1652.

Sir Marmaduke Langdale (1598–1661) was a Catholic Yorkshireman recognized by both sides in the Civil War as an outstanding cavalry commander. He served under George Goring until 1644. After the battle of Marston Moor he commanded the Northern Horse. After his capture by the Parliamentarians in 1648 he escaped from captivity in Nottingham Castle disguised as one of his captors, and then, dressed as a milkmaid, reached the Humber, which he swam; he then assumed the guise of a clergyman to make his way to London before going abroad.

Sir Henry Slingsby (1602–58) was a Yorkshireman who served in the Low Countries in the 1630s. In 1642 he commanded the Trained Bands of York and then raised his own regiment of foot to serve under the duke of Newcastle. He was with the Northern Horse at Leicester and at Naseby. He stayed with Charles I after that disaster and was finally sent home in 1646. In hiding he completed his *Diary*. He was a leader of the unsuccessful rising of 1655 and was beheaded in London in June 1658.

John, Lord Belasyse (1614–89) was one of the first to join Charles at the outbreak of the war. He was captured by his cousins, the Fairfaxes, in April 1644 but was exchanged and was with the King's Lifeguard at Naseby. His account was written some years later.

Richard Symonds (1617–92?) served as a trooper in the King's Lifeguard of Horse and kept a diary in which he records not only the events of the war but also his researches into the churches of England. His account is factual rather than analytical.

PARLIAMENTARIAN COMMANDERS

Sir Thomas Fairfax (1612–71), son of Ferdinando, Lord Fairfax, was born in Denton in North Yorkshire. He had some limited military experience gained in the Low Countries. In 1639 he served under Charles I against the Scots, but joined the Parliamentary forces when the Civil War broke out in 1642. His father commanded Parliament's Northern Army. They were defeated at Adwalton Moor, outside Bradford, in 1643. Sir Thomas, together with Oliver Cromwell, checked the Royalist encroachment from Newark by beating them at Winceby in October. The next year father and son joined to besiege York and brought Prince Rupert rushing to the rescue of the Royalists, precipitating the battle of Marston Moor on 2 July. On the creation of the New Model Army in 1645, Sir Thomas, neither a member of Parliament nor a peer, was the obvious choice for Captain-General – its leader. In a matter of months Fairfax moulded the new formations, more than half composed of veteran soldiers, into a disciplined force.

Sir Thomas Fairfax, from Sprigge's *Anglia Rediviva*. (Naseby Battlefield Project)

Oliver Cromwell (1599–1658) was a country gentleman of modest means and no military experience who represented Cambridge in the Long Parliament and raised a troop of horse when war broke out. He was a deeply religious man who recruited similar men to his service. By 1644, as Lieutenant-General of the Horse of the Eastern Association, he was demonstrating his abilities as a commander at Marston Moor, where he defeated the Royalist right wing and then joined Fairfax to rout Goring's horse. In spite of being a member of Parliament he was appointed Lieutenant-General in the New Model Army and commanded the horse at Naseby. His subsequent career showed him to be one of the greatest generals Britain has ever produced.

Henry Ireton (1611–51) was without military experience when the war began, but in June 1642 raised a troop of cavalry and fought at the battle of Edgehill, participating again at Gainsborough in 1643 under Cromwell. He then became Cromwell's deputy-governor in the Isle of Ely. He served as quartermaster-general to the earl of Manchester in Yorkshire in the Marston Moor campaign of summer 1644 and at Newbury that October. Cromwell appointed Ireton Commissary-General of Horse at Naseby. In June 1646 he married Cromwell's eldest daughter, Bridget. In 1650 he was made Cromwell's deputy in Ireland and died of a fever at Limerick.

Philip Skippon (*c*.1600–60) returned in 1638 from some 25 years' professional soldiering in Denmark, Germany and the Low Countries and took up the post of Captain-Leader, i.e. training officer, to the Society of the Artillery Garden in London. He was appointed to the command of the London Trained Bands as Sergeant-Major-General of the City of London in 1642 and led his force, alongside the earl of Essex,

to outface the king at Turnham Green in November that year. Essex
made him Sergeant-Major-General of his army. When the New Model
Army was formed, Skippon was chosen for the same post and did
sterling work in uniting the old and new troops into an efficient force.

Edward Montagu (1625–72) raised a regiment in the Parliamentarian
cause in 1643 and fought at Marston Moor. At Naseby his regiment was
in the front line and did well. After taking part in the storming of Bristol
he became a member of Parliament.

Sir Hardress Waller (*c.*1604–66) served in Holland before the war and in
Munster until the formation of a regiment which Sir William Waller's
major-general, James Holborne, declined to lead because, as a Scot, he
would not serve in the New Model Army. He was wounded when
storming Basing House in October 1645.

Thomas Pride (*c.*1605–58) is said to have been a foundling and a
brewer's drayman, an allegation enjoyed by Royalist propagandists in
the rhyme '...But yet for all his militarie Art / At Naseby fight he let a
Brewer's f*rt.' He in fact commanded the regiment of the wounded
Colonel Edward Harley in the reserve and acquitted himself well.

John Okey (1606–62) rose to the rank of major in Sir Arthur Haselrigge's Regiment of Horse in Sir William Waller's army (although the source for this may be unreliable). On 1 March 1645 Fairfax proposed to Parliament that the dragoons should be formed into a regiment and it was so resolved two days later. Okey was given the command, taking over John Lilburne's regiment near Abingdon on 30 April. Okey's Regiment had an establishment of 1,000 in ten companies, but when he led them at Naseby they numbered no more than 676 officers and men. His letter about Naseby was written within two or three days of the battle.

The Reverend Joshua Sprigge (1618–84) was born in Banbury and educated in Edinburgh, becoming a clergyman. He was chaplain to Thomas Fairfax and was possibly with the Parliamentarian train at Naseby. His book *Anglia Rediviva* was published in 1647 and gives an account of the actions, some of which he may have witnessed, of the New Model Army. It contains Robert Streeter's engraving of the battle; a pictogram made in the style conventional at that time rather than a map in modern terms. It was an official publication inasmuch as Parliament later voted the funds to cover the artist's loss on the work.

Frances Rushworth was secretary to Fairfax and wrote a long letter about the battle of Naseby from Market Harborough at 2.00am the next morning.

Captain Edward Wogan (d. 1654) was an officer with Okey's Dragoons and wrote of his experiences some years later.

Colonel Thomas Rainsborough (or Rainborowe) (*c.*1610–48) was a sea captain, possibly born in Massachusetts, whose sister married, first, John Winthrop who became governor of the colony and, after his death, John Coggon of Boston, Massachusetts. He raised a foot regiment which had other men from Massachusetts among its officers: Lieutenant-Colonel Israel Stoughton, Major Nehemiah Bourne and Captain John Leverett, who become the colony's governor in 1673, but their presence at Naseby is uncertain. Rainsborough's brother, William, served as a captain in Sheffield's Regiment of Horse.

Bulstrode Whitelocke (1605–76) was member of Parliament for Marlow, Buckinghamshire, before the war and attempted to stay safe in the middle ground of politics. He compiled *Memorials of English Affairs*, which was eventually published in 1853 and is largely drawn from secondary sources.

Nathaniel Whetham (1604–68) was made governor of Northampton in 1642.

Sir Samuel Luke (1603–70) was governor of Newport Pagnell and conducted a substantial correspondence with his father in London and with other officers of the Parliamentarian armies. His letterbooks have been published.

OPPOSING ARMIES

EQUIPMENT, FORMATIONS AND TACTICS

By 1645 the training-ground-manual prescriptions familiar to all at the outbreak of war three years earlier had been tested, modified and recast to suit the particular circumstances of war in England. The revised and new manuals reflected this.

The foot

The traditional formation of foot was a block of pikemen flanked by musketeers (or 'shot'). It was the task of the pike to protect the shot from attack by enemy horse, but in close country, strongly hedged, the shot could certainly look after themselves and even in open fields the musketeers could give a good account of themselves unless assaulted by formed troops of cavalry. As the war proceeded, musket became dominant as Sir James Turner remarked in *Pallas Armata*: '...Companies how strong or weak soever were divided into three parts, two thirds whereof were pikemen, and one third musqueteers; thereafter the Musquet craved half the game and got it ... very soon the musqueteers challenged ... leaving but one third for the pikemen...'

The government attempted to bring order to the impractical diversity of firearms in 1630. The Council of War set out 'Orders for the general uniformatie of all sortes of armes both for horse and foote' which Howard Blackmore summarizes as follows:

	Barrel length	Overall length	Bore
Pistol	18in.	26in.	24
Arquebus	30in.	45in.	17
Carbine or Petronel	30in.	45in.	24
Musket	48in.	62in.	12
Caliver	39in.	54in.	17

(Bore: Bullets to the pound of lead, 'rowleing in'.)
Modern calibres are based on this ancient system, and a 12-bore gun is 0.729in./18.5mm in diameter, a 17-bore gun is 0.649in./16.5mm and a 24-bore gun is 0.579in./14.7mm.

Various notes suggest that the pistol and the arquebus were wheellock weapons. In 1639 it was found that a pistol of barrel length 16in. was as accurate as one of even 20in., but the standard was left alone. Ordnance officers also recommended that a musket barrel should be 42in., lessening the weight to something between 10lb and 11lb, and that the recoil should be reduced by using a powder charge of half, rather than two-thirds, of the bullet weight.

The standard musket was a matchlock. It was fired by bringing the glowing end of a length of slow-match cord into contact with powder in a flash-pan, which in turn ignited the charge in the barrel of the piece. The match was hempen, if available, and was boiled in either wine vinegar or a solution of saltpetre. It was a simple system, and very reliable as long as its constituents were dry. The disadvantages of match were the difficulty of keeping it dry in bad weather, the glow it made in the dark, and arranging for its supply. Saltpetre had to be imported and huge quantities of the stuff were needed to furnish the needs of any significant body of men, which was both troublesome and expensive. Therefore a proportion of firelocks which used flint ignition were issued, sparing the consumption of match, and avoiding the risk of accidental ignition of gunpowder stores by wind-blown sparks or revelation of a guard by match-glow. They were, however, more expensive to manufacture and prone to misfire, much as a flint-ignition cigarette lighter could require more than a single thumb-flick to make it light.

The powder was carried in a collar of bandoliers, each with between six and 16 bottles or 'boxes' with the appropriate charge of powder. The bullets were carried in a bag and were often transferred to the mouth to assist speedy reloading, while a flask for powder to prime the flash-pan was becoming a rarity at this time. The manufacture of powder bottles was another expense and the Oxford Army seems to have been issued with powder bags, to be slung from a belt that also supported a sword. Loose powder was impractical and dangerous, so cartridges must have been used. These were paper packets which were torn open to allow the musketeer to pour the charge down the barrel and use the empty paper as wadding to hold the bullet in place.

The weapons had the handicaps of low muzzle velocity, variable bullet-to-barrel fit ('windage'), and a heavy bullet with significant wind-resistance. Over a distance of 120 yards the bullet dropped by 5ft, so a good marksman might score a hit at 100 yards, a volley might hurt an enemy formation at 200 yards, but at 300 yards firing was virtually futile.

The pikeman was equipped with a weapon made of ash with a metal head, either a broad spearhead, which was found wanting in practice, or a smaller, four-sided spike fastened to the shaft with cheeks, strips of metal, running down the shaft to prevent the head being cut off. The length was about 16ft, although some authorities say 18ft, and all agree that men were to be prevented from cutting off a foot or two to lighten them. The pikeman wore a helmet but by 1645 some had even abandoned the heavy back- and breastplates. The *tassets,* which protected the thighs, and the *gorget,* which guarded the throat, were rarely seen even early in the war. For close-quarter fighting he had a sword.

The horse

In 1644 John Vernon, a Parliamentary cavalryman serving, perhaps, in the army of the earl of Essex, wrote *The Young Horseman.* In this book he describes the cavalryman of that time and army and thus not necessarily the Ironside of the New Model. He begins with the trooper's mount:

> *First make choise of a nimble and able Horse of a convenient Stature, of 15 handfulls high, sad coloured, as black, brown, cheasnut [in order to reduce visibility to the enemy] … let not the neck of your spurs be overlong [lest they get caught up in the stirrup of the man next to you]…*

a   b

NASEBY BREAST AND BACK

(a) **This breast and back, or cuirass, was made during the Civil War and bears two makers' marks, those of John Hill and William Dawston, both London armourers. It was sent to Nigel Carren for restoration and reproduction of the shoulder straps. It fits Nigel, on whom it can be seen** (b) **that any larger breastplate would inhibit arm and leg mobility, taking into account that it was worn over a buff coat, that is, a leather garment made of material some** $^1/_{10}$**in. thick. These items are from the collection of Captain Andrzej B. Gawlik, US Marine Corps. (John Kliene)**

The armament was a sword 'of a middle length, sharpe pointed and stiffe' because a long sword was harder to handle and not needed by a mounted man. He advises against cartridges for the pistol charge as trotting tended to shake out the powder, and suggests a flask instead. The firearms should be two pistols and a carbine. A poll-axe was, he says, 'very necessarie' for employment against cuirassiers, the heavy, armoured horsemen. There should be 'an Iron or brasse chain for false Reins covered over with leather, for if your other Reins should chance to be cut, those will then stand you in good stead...'

The cuirassier's armour and equipment was 'chiefly defensive' and receives a brief description, for by this time the expense and weight of the armour had rendered this type of cavalry almost redundant. Vernon assumes that the 'Harbuyusers' were the standard form of cavalry. The defensive arms were a 'Caske or Head-peece', that is a helmet, and back- and breastplate worn over a buff coat. The offensive arms were 'a good Harquebus, or a Carbine hanging on his right side by a sweble [swivel], a flask and a Carthareg [cartridge] case, spannere, and to [two] good fire-lock pistols in houlsters.' And, as above, the poll-axe and stiff sword. The horse at Naseby were, for the most part, armed with sword and pistol only.

The dragoon's arming, Vernon continues, 'is only offensive, having a good fire lock musket something awider bore then ordinary hanging in a belt by a sweble at his side, with a good sword and ordinary horse, it being only to expedite his march, for he must perform his service on foot...' They rode ten abreast and when they fought nine dismounted, throwing their reins over the neck of the horse next to them so the tenth could hold the horses of a whole rank. The lack of 'defensive arming' meant that these troops were without helmets or body armour.

Fighting tactics

The publication of *Militarie Discipline or the Young Artillery-man* by William Barriffe in 1635 put yet another manual into a market that had been

Try yo.̊ Match.

9

*How he shall handsomely trye
the Match with the Thumb &
second finger, that he may presently set it eyther higher or
lower, longer or shorter.*

Hold vp yo.̊ Musket & Present

11

*Then hauing layd the Musket
in ỹ Rest. keeping allwaies the
mouth of it somewhat vpwards,
setting the left legge before, &
the Rest somewhat foreward.*

Giue fire

12

*To present well and giue fire, ỹ
musket in the Rest held by ỹ left
hand, the right elbow somewhat vp,
& turning the body a little to the
left side, the left knee bowed the
Right legge straight out, ỹ it may
be held and shot of the surer.*

Musket exercises from *The Art of Martiall Discipline* showing part of the firing sequence with a musket rest in use. By 1645 the shorter, lighter musket was in use and the rest became redundant. (Perry Miniatures)

supplied with drill-books charting the evolution of warfare and the use of weapons since Jacob de Gheyn's *The Exercise of Arms* in 1607. Although it appeared in a sixth edition in 1661, much of what it contains reveals the formations approved at the outbreak of the war, and here musketeers are shown as drawn up four men wide and eight men deep on either side of a block of pikemen eight wide and eight deep, a formation of equal numbers of pike and shot. In such a formation the musketeers fired by single ranks, the front rank firing and then turning to the rear of the formation to reload while the second rank fired and so on. However, a much more aggressive approach had already been introduced by the Swedish king and general Gustavus Adolphus, firing by salvee when two or more ranks fired at the same time. Sir James Turner, who served in the Swedish army, advocated the tactic thus:

> *For thereby you pour as much lead in your enemies bosom at one time as you do the other way at two several times, and thereby you do them more mischief, you quail, daunt, and astonish them three times more, for one long and continual crack of thunder is more terrible and dreadful to mortals than ten interrupted and several ones.*

It is notable that Sir James speaks more of the terror inspired by the noise than the injury done by the bullets, but that is a fair reflection of the efficacy of small-arms fire at the time.

A description in *The Swedish Intelligencer* is specific on how the Scots carried out the salvee at the first battle of Breitenfeld on 17 September 1631:

> *...the formost ranke falling upon their knees; the second stooping forward and the third ranke standing right up, and all giuing fire together; they powerd so much lead at one instant in amongst the enemies horse that their ranckes were much broken by it.*

25

Colonel Walter Slingsby fought at Cheriton on 29 March 1644 and it is clear from his description of holding off a Parliamentarian attack that the Royalist shot fired in this manner:

> They immediately try'd the second charge in which Captain Herbert of my Lord Hoptons Regiment was slaine, with a fresh body and were againe repulsed, and soe againe the third time, the foote keeping their ground in a close body, not firing until within two pikes length, and then three rankes att a time, after turning up the butt end of their muskets, charging their pikes, and standing close, preserv'd themselves, and slew many of the enemy.

Once his weapon had been discharged, the musketeer was likely to find himself hand-to-hand with his adversary when, as Slingsby mentions, he reversed the firearm to use it as a club. By this time the formations were usually six men deep.

The traditional role of the pikeman was to withstand horse, the shot sheltering beneath the bristling hedge of pikes and amongst their ranks. The menace of massed pikes to cavalry is easy to imagine and the classic response of the foot was described by Elton:

> In my opinion the best way of opposing the horse charge is that which we learned of our ever honoured Captain, Major Henry Tillier, in the Military Garden; which was, Files closing to the midst to their closest order, insomuch as there was not above half a foot interval of ground between File and File, the pikes Porting, and after closing their Ranks forwards so close, that they locked themselves one with another, and then charged on.

It can be questioned whether the pikemen were needed at all. At the battle of the Dunes on 14 June 1658 the duke of York found, once his horse had broken into a battalion of foot, that the enemy fought on with the butt-ends of muskets and he was himself unhorsed and fortunate to land a blow with his sword before being clubbed. Thus, if the foot kept their heads in the crisis, they might do very well against disorganized horse.

The pikemen might also fight enemies similarly armed, and the phrase 'push of pike' conjures a vision of mutual skewering. There is no evidence of this taking place, for both sides were armoured when the term was coined and, lacking momentum, pushing was indeed what took place. There are accounts of men being thrust onto their backs by a stronger opponent, but not run through. Indeed, at close quarters aggression was pursued with the sword, and it seems probable that the whippy pike was such a nuisance when moving fast that it was jettisoned in favour of the edged weapon – hoping the sword had not been rendered useless by its usual employment: cutting firewood.

Very often the regiments lacked enough men to form up in textbook style. Company and regimental units were absorbed into larger formations to give musket blocks and battalia, that is pike and musket formations, as might be desirable. In order to facilitate this, battle plans were carefully drawn up at the commencement of a campaign and, particularly in the case of those of the Royalist engineer Sir Bernard de

Gomme, they are what we see when the plan of the dispositions at a given battle is produced. It is worth remembering that they show the intention, not necessarily the outcome in the field.

The cavalry's formation for fighting in open country, such as existed at Naseby, was described by Vernon thus:

> *...all the Troops are to be drawn into battalia, each being not above three deepe, likewise each troop must be at least a hundred paces distance behind each other for the better avoiding of disorder, those troops that are to give the first charge being drawn up into battail as before, are to be at their close order, every left hand mans right knee must be close locked under his right hand mans left ham ... In this order they are to advance towards the Enemy with an easie pace, firing their Carbines at a convenient distance ... the troops are to charge the Enemy in full career, but in good order with their swords fastned with a Riband or the like to their wrists ... still keeping in close order close locked...*

The situation of two troops of equal strength charging one another is mentioned. The reader's troop (the intended victor) is advised:

> *...sodainly to divide your Troop in the middle: on [one] Flank from the other, and so the Enemie being in his full career, must either passé through and effect little, or else stopping sodainly disorder his own Troops, and the[r]eby give you a fit occasion to wheel both your Flanks inward, to charge him in the Reer.*

Of encounters with infantry, Vernon instructs that the horse should only attack in 'Champaigne ground, cleere of Trees, Hedges, Ditches or the like...' Even so, it would be necessary to divide the troop into three, one to charge the foot in front, while the others moved against a flank and in the rear.

In general terms the horse were first used against each other with the opposing bodies massed into a solid, moving wall to smash into their enemy, having perhaps attempted to break their formation with carbine and pistol shot, but actually meeting with drawn swords. In broken fighting, when formations of foot had become disorganized, the cavalry could get in amongst the infantry with sword and pistol, but attacking properly formed foot was not advised.

As a rule, it appears, the safest course of action for any soldier was to keep formation. In encounters that ended with no clear-cut victor, casualties were small and fatalities very few. If you lost, surrender was wise; the most dangerous thing to do was to run away. To disengage with a fighting retreat when necessary was both prudent and honourable.

THE NEW MODEL ARMY

On 11 January 1645 the Commons resolved to raise a new army of ten regiments of horse, one of dragoons and 12 of foot. The money needed would be raised by a monthly assessment on the 17 counties of the Midlands, East Anglia and the South which lay within Parliamentary control.

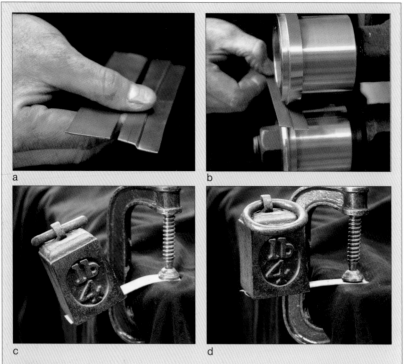

STEPPING

The steps in armour have been erroneously attributed to an attempt to simulate segmentation on *tassets* (thigh protectors) or pot-tails. The true purpose is shown by comparing two samples (a). The process of stepping is demonstrated by Nigel Carren who is cranking a 1in.-wide sample of steel through wheels that give it a step of ³/₅₀in. (b). A 4lb weight bends the unstepped sample easily (c), while the stepped sample under the same pressure remains rigid (d). Cranked out armour, as 17th-century armour was often called at the time, produced stepped armour – strong, rigid protection, mass-produced, adding strength without adding weight. (John Kliene)

The horse

The cavalry regiments of the time had an establishment of six troops of, as a rule, 60 men. There were many deviations in practice. Oliver Cromwell's 'Ironsides' had 14 troops and thus were able to furnish the men for Whalley's Regiment and for Fairfax's Regiment, with men to spare. The New Model Army adopted the structure of the Eastern Association, with a modification giving each regiment six troops of about 100 men. The final ordinance establishing the New Model Army was passed on 11 February, at which time an 11th regiment of horse was added.

Four cavalry regiments came from Essex's army, five from Manchester's (the Eastern Association), one from Waller's and one each from the provincial forces of Kent and Lincolnshire.

The dragoons

The resolution of the Commons on 11 January stated 'there shall be raised, for this Army, a Thousand Dragoons, to be in Ten Companies.' A preliminary list of colonels approved by the Commons on 21 January makes no mention of the dragoons, either by naming a commander or as a regiment. This was not unusual at the time, as dragoons usually

Three postures for pikemen from *The Art of Martiall Discipline*, an English Militia officer's notebook of the early 17th century. (Perry Miniatures)

operated as independent companies, sometimes attached to a cavalry regiment. It may, therefore, have been assumed that each of the ten companies would attach to one of the ten regiments of horse initially ordained. On 1 March Sir Thomas Fairfax wrote to the Commons proposing, *inter alia*, that the dragoons should be formed into a regiment and on 3 March the report of the Commons debates says: 'Resolved, &c. That the Dragooners shall be formed into a Regiment. The Colonel and Officers of the Dragoons were all reported and approved.'

The provenance of the officers is uncertain as two lists, one from the *Journals of the House of Lords* and the other from Joshua Sprigge's *Anglia Rediviva*, are available. The latter shows that four officers, including Colonel John Okey, were from Waller's army, four from the Eastern Association and two from elsewhere, unspecified. Thomas Fairfax issued a commission on 1 April 1645 to pay John Farmer £20 towards the raising of a company of dragoons, and his, presumably new, company is shown in pay warrants as having a strength of 105 officers and men shortly before the battle. The strength of Okey's Regiment altogether is given as 676 officers and men.

The foot

The regiment of foot in the New Model Army was planned to number 1,200 men in ten companies. The companies were not of equal size. The colonel's had 200 men, the lieutenant-colonel's 160, the sergeant-major's 140 and the seven captains commanded 100 each. The establishment was rarely attained in real life and a regiment more often numbered fewer than 700, and often something between 500 and 300. The proportion of musketeers to pikemen was intended to be 2:1, but again that might not be the case in practice. While officers and horse were available in appropriate numbers from the previous Parliamentary armies, infantry were in short supply with 3,048 from the earl of Essex's army, 3,578 from the earl of Manchester's Eastern Association and a mere 600 from Sir William Waller's; 7,226 in all. New levies were required to make up the

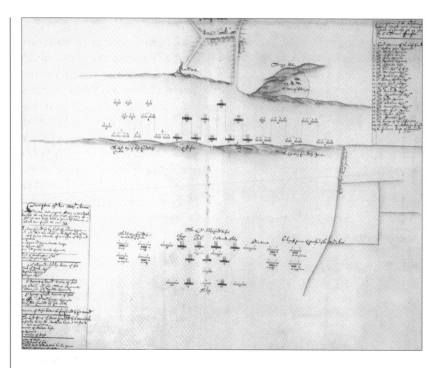

Sir Bernard de Gomme drew up battle plans for the Royalists, and this historical plan is based upon one made well before the battle took place. It includes the positions of the Parliamentarian forces beyond a hill, perhaps taken from Streeter, and the Sulby Hedges. Behind the hedges are a number of closes, in one of which Colonel Okey took up a position. It remains a diagram rather than a map. (Westaway Collection)

numbers. In April 5,650 muskets and 2,000 pikes were ordered to equip them, which suggests a musket to pike ratio of 3:1 and when Essex's men were re-armed after their defeat at Lostwithiel a ratio of 6:1 is recorded. In the event something in the region of 4:1 may have been the outcome overall.

The foot regiments were sourced as follows: five from Essex's army, four from the Eastern Association, one from Waller's and one from Kent.

Strength

The numbers actually being paid just before Naseby have been calculated from the State Papers in the National Archives by David Blackmore. He computes that the total of the horse was 5,478, of foot 8,624 and of dragoons 676. However, two small foot regiments, Lloyd's and Ingoldsby's, were at Taunton and the foot therefore may have numbered 8,468. The horse, on the other hand, was augmented by Colonel John Fiennes's of the Midland Association with perhaps 200 men and by the Associated Horse with another 400 or so. Their total thus rises to 6,078 and that of the army as a whole to 15,222 in theory and, allowing for sickness and other minor depletions by mid-June, that could have fallen by 10 per cent to about 13,700. The *Scottish Dove* reported that, at Newport Pagnell, the figures were 7,031 foot and 3,014 horse, the latter increased later by Cromwell's and Vermuyden's to a total of between 5,500 and 6,000 according to Stuart Reid; this gives a total of 13,000 or so, which, eroded as above, leaves 11,700.

THE ROYALIST 'OXFORD' ARMY

In contrast to their enemies, the winter of 1644–45 had not seen a more coherent structure or chain of command introduced to the Royalist forces. Their military units were of no regular size or structure and often comprised a piecemeal collection of forces, hence their army structure cannot be outlined so clearly as that of the Parliamentarian army, which itself was formed of units of differing strength. For this reason we cannot assume that any one regiment pitched against another would be fighting an equal force. The main force, commanded by the king, was the Oxford Army, while Prince Maurice, Charles Gerard and Lord Goring were leading forces in the South and West. The revised version of the battle plan of early June, made later by Sir Bernard de Gomme, Rupert's Walloon engineer, shows the army drawn up in tertia of two or three regiments and is the basis for the Order of Battle shown here. The plan is broadly descriptive but not exhaustive; it omits some regiments known to have been present, at least in part, as noted below.

Strength

Not only is it difficult to establish the numbers of men that made up this force, but it is also hard to estimate the proportion of shot to pike present. It would seem that only the 500 men of the Duke of York's were in the conventional 2:1 shot-to-pike ratio. The rest of Astley's tertia, about 850 men, had a higher proportion of shot to pike, perhaps 4:1. Within Bard's Tertia, Thomas's battalion of some 500 men had about the same ratio, whilst the 700 men in Gerard's were nearly all garrison troops and would have been almost entirely shot. In Lisle's tertia, Lisle's and St George's regiments comprised 450 men with a shot-to-pike ratio of perhaps 4:1 and the Shrewsbury Foot, 500 men with muskets. These three tertia had a strength of about 3,500 men. In addition there were the King's Lifeguard of Foot, 200 men, and Prince Rupert's Bluecoats,

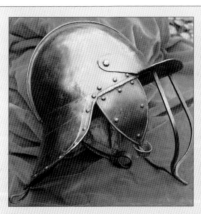
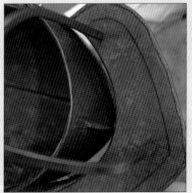

a   b

TROOPER'S THREE-BAR POT
In this reproduction pot made by Nigel Carren, the ridge on the skull is the join of two halves which not only speeds manufacture but also adds strength and rigidity. The tail is stepped, which also adds rigidity, and is fitted with a carrying loop of leather (a). The 'fall' and three-bar face-cage clicks into the closed position when it passes over the skull ridge to a flat section on the brow (b), and thus remains steadily in place as the wearer moves or rides. The dark colour is obtained by heating it to cherry-red and allowing it to cool to grey before immersing it in oil, thus rendering it water- and rust-resistant as well as reducing its light reflection. A padded lining makes it reasonably comfortable to wear. (John Kliene)

500 strong, in reserve with a conventional 2:1 shot-to-pike ratio and two units of commanded musketeers, each 200 strong, with the cavalry. The total infantry strength can thus be computed at 4,600 men. Further, while the reserve had a conventional make-up, the main body of the Oxford Army had a shot to pike ratio of 5:1, some 2,925 shot to 575 pike – a situation that must have had an impact on its tactical behaviour.

The wings of the Royalist horse were, in the Swedish style, supported by shot. The right wing at Naseby had 1,710 horse with 200 shot. The left wing under Sir Marmaduke Langdale had the same number in three divisions. The centre included, in the second line, Thomas Howard's three divisions, a total of 880 horse.

The reserve of horse comprised the King's Lifeguard and the Newark Horse, perhaps 1,300 in all, bringing the total of horse to 5,590 and the Royalist force as a whole to some 10,200 men. Stuart Reid, relying on figures cited in the contemporary *Diary of the Marches of the Royal Army* by Richard Symonds, who served in the Lifeguard, suggests that the horse numbered 5,450 and the foot 5,000, a total of 10,450.

From the listings it is clear that the Royalist army was fashioned from the fragments of numerous regiments that had been mauled in previous years, and that many of these were present in much-reduced strength. The Shrewsbury Foot, for example, was based on the survivors of the defeat at Monmouth with, no doubt, new men added. Some units, such as Rupert's Bluecoat Regiment of Foot, appear to have been preserved as coherent formations. Although the experience of the men was substantial, command and control and thus the ability to fight as a unit may have been adversely affected and the extent to which morale and loyalty were preserved is open to conjecture. In broken battle conditions, when larger formations may have been dispersed, a small body of musketeers coalescing around their commanding officer could prove to be a disproportionately formidable unit and, given leaders of experience, such bodies could give each other covering fire in a fighting retreat.

Another portrait by van Dyke of Charles I. He is wearing armour, implying a more martial character than his sensitive features suggest. (Copyright Akg-images)

ORDERS OF BATTLE

THE BATTLE OF NASEBY, 14 JUNE 1645

PARLIAMENTARY FORCES (after Foard, from Streeter)
Sir Thomas Fairfax

Right wing of horse
Lieutenant-General of Horse Oliver Cromwell
 The General's (Fairfax's) Lifeguard
 Sir Robert Pye's Regiment
 Colonel Edward Whalley's Regiment
 Colonel Thomas Sheffield's Division
 Colonel John Fiennes's Regiment
 Colonel Edward Rossiter's Regiment
 The Associated Horse

Foot
Sergeant-Major-General Philip Skippon
 Sir Thomas Fairfax's Regiment
 Colonel Edward Montagu's Regiment
 Colonel John Pickering's Regiment
 Sir Hardress Waller's Regiment
 Sergeant-Major-General Philip Skippon's Regiment
 Lieutenant-Colonel Thomas Pride's Regiment
 Colonel Robert Hammond's Regiment
 Colonel Thomas Rainsborough's Regiment
 Lieutenant-Colonel Pride's Rearguard

Left wing of horse
Commissary-General of Horse Henry Ireton
 Colonel John Butler's Regiment
 Colonel Bartholemew Vermuyden's Regiment
Commissary-General Henry Ireton's Regiment
 Colonel Nathaniel Rich's Regiment
 Colonel Charles Fleetwood's Regiment
 The Associated Horse

Other units
 The Artillery Train
 The Forlorn Hope of Musketeers
 Colonel Okey's Dragoons

ROYALIST FORCES (after Foard, from de Gomme)
His Majesty, Charles, King of England, Scotland and Ireland
Prince Rupert, Count Palatine of the Rhine and Duke of Bavaria

Right wing of horse
Prince Maurice
Prince Rupert's and Prince Maurice's Lifeguards
Prince Rupert's Regiment
The Queen's and Prince Maurice's Regiments
The Earl of Northampton's Regiment
Sir William Vaughan's Regiment

Foot
Lord Astley

Sir Bernard Astley's Tertia of Foot
The Duke of York's Regiment
Sir Edward Hopton's Regiment
Sir Richard Page's Regiment
Sir Henry Bard's Tertia
    Sir Henry Bard's Regiment and the Queen's Lifeguard
    Sir John Owen's and Colonel Radcliffe Gerard's Regiments
Sir George Lisle's Tertia
    Sir George Lisle's and Colonel St George's Regiments
    The Shrewsbury Foot [Broughton's, Tillier's, Hunks's, Warren's and Gibson's
    Regiments]
Three Divisions of Horse
    Bagot's and Leveson's
    Colonel Thomas Howard's

Left wing of horse
Sir Marmaduke Langdale
    The Northern Horse, three divisions under Sir Marmaduke Langdale
    Sir Horatio Carey's Regiment
    The Northern Horse, one division under Sir William Blackiston

Reserve
    The Newark Horse
    The King's Lifeguard of Foot
    The King's Lifeguard of Horse
    Prince Rupert's Bluecoat Regiment of Foot

OPPOSING PLANS

The reformation of the Parliamentarian army did not remove it from the control of the Committee of Both Kingdoms. The committee drew its membership from both houses of Parliament and had been set up in February 1644 as what today would be called a war cabinet, to take strategic control of the war. The extent to which it became involved in tactical or operational matters varied. On the formation of the New Model Army it exercised close control, sending armies, regiments and, indeed, individuals about their tasks. The committee, which included experienced military men such as Sir William Waller and the earls of Manchester and of Essex, met daily. Between 2 and 9 June, for example, a period crucial to the campaign, Manchester and Waller attended every day and Essex missed only one day.

The Royalist strategy was the province of Charles I himself, drawing on the advice of a covey of courtiers with limited military knowledge, a few select individuals rather better qualified and, from time to time, a more formal council of war at which the principal field commanders were present. Prince Rupert, although commander-in-chief of the army, was not the most influential of the king's advisers, but he was supported by the duke of Richmond and by the secretary of state Sir Edward Nicholas. Chief amongst his detractors were George, Lord Digby, another of the secretaries of state, Sir Edward Walker, who was Charles's Secretary at War, and John Ashburnham, the Paymaster General. The king's deliberations appear to have been chiefly affected by whomever he last consulted.

PARLIAMENTARY PLANS

Given the recent birth of the New Model Army and the need to allow time for it to settle into being an effective force, two considerations dominated the committee's modest offensive policy in the spring of 1645. First was the spoiling of efforts to pull together Royalist forces around Oxford, and for this purpose Cromwell was positioned near the city in April. Second was the relief of Taunton, which, if it fell to the Royalists, would no longer inhibit the increase of their forces in the West and the reinforcement of the king's army at Oxford and their exploitation of the resources of the region, and for this purpose Fairfax took the New Model Army westwards. The defensive policy was centred on the territory of the Eastern Association, crucial as it was to their supply, and this would overtake aggressive schemes if a threat was perceived. The major strategic objective had been to combine with Lord Leven's Scots, then in Yorkshire, and surround the king at Oxford, but the lesser actions distracted them from the plan. Moreover, the Scots were concerned to protect their heartlands against Royalist operations in their own country, and therefore were unwilling to risk a move southwards.

ROYALIST PLANS

The strategic vision of the Royalists was also unfocused. Lord Goring was conducting spoiling operations in the South, beating up Parliamentarian troops in Dorset, for example, and Sir Richard Grenville was set on removing his enemies from Taunton in order to build his western army into a war-winning force. When Grenville was wounded the policy of his successor was merely to blockade the town and the initiative was lost. Meanwhile the princes, Maurice and Rupert, concerned themselves with regaining ground in South Wales and the Marches.

The king left Oxford on 7 May, still without a grand strategy, and a council of war was held at Stow-on-the-Wold. They were cheered by the successes of James Graham, Marquess of Montrose in Scotland, and entertained hopes of the Scottish threat in the North being drawn off by the war in the Northern Kingdom, and they were also comforted by the belief that the 'New Noddle' army would prove to be a flawed formation. But they had yet to agree a plan. It was soon decided that the Eastern Association was too tough a nut to crack, but choosing between the alternatives of mounting a campaign in the West Country and of regaining the North of England was not easily done. In the end it was decided to do both in part. Lord Goring was to return to the siege of Taunton, with instructions to rejoin the king when so commanded, and the rest would proceed to the relief of Chester. And after that they'd think again.

In early May neither side had a clear strategic objective and both were content to divide their forces to pursue small actions at unrelated locations. The Committee of Both Kingdoms was already acting to secure Parliament's home territory and Prince Rupert wrote to Colonel William Legge to do the same for his royal master.

> *Sir,*
> *You are immediately upon sight hereof to take into your charge and command, as Commander in Cheife, all your Inferior and subordinate garrisons to, and neare, the Citty of Oxford, the garrison of Banbury excepted, all which are to obey, and receive orders from you. Ffurther requiring all Comanders Governours, and officers of all other his Majestys Garrisons, to be aiding, and assisting unto you, upon all occasions, whensoever they shalbe required by you for the defence of the Citty & county of Oxford. Hereof you and they respectively are not to faile.*
> *Given at Burford this 7th of May 1645*
> *Rupert*

Within this flimsy strategic framework the decisive campaign of the English Civil War began, but perhaps the outcome would be determined by the ease with which one side or the other could fall back on a policy of great simplicity. For the Royalists, lacking the resources to attack the territory of the Eastern Association, it was impossible to identify a single, simple objective. For the Committee of Both Kingdoms it was instinctive to fall back on targeting the Royalist heartland: Oxford.

THE CAMPAIGN

PARLIAMENTARY PRELIMINARIES

Oliver Cromwell was ordered to begin his operations around Oxford on 20 April, instructed by the Committee of Both Kingdoms to prevent Prince Maurice moving artillery to Rupert at Hereford. He left Watlington with 1,500 horse on 23 April and discovered that the earl of Northampton was billeted at Islip, 5 miles north of Oxford, so he made to attack him. Northampton had been forewarned and had slipped away, but returned the following day and got the worst of the encounter. Richard Symonds, a trooper in the King's Lifeguard, recorded in his diary:

> *Thursday, April 24, 1645. Cromwell's horse and dragoons ruined some of our horse that quartered about Islip ... 21 buried in Islip. 18 men buried ... over against Kidlington; and this day they demanded the delivery up of Blechington, a howse belonging to Sir Thomas Coghill, wherin Colonel Windibanke had 200 foot, sans workes, and provision only for two or three days... About two or three of the clock, Friday morning, the colonel valiantly gave up the house and all his armes, &c., besides 50 horse that came thither for shelter; and this without a shott.*

Blechington (today called Blechingdon) lies some 3 miles north-north-east of Islip and the horse escaping from the previous day's action had taken refuge there. Cromwell's sweep continued anticlockwise to Bampton, between Witney and Faringdon, where he got the better of Sir William Vaughan's foot, capturing 300 of them in a brisk skirmish, and finished on 30 April with a rather optimistic summons to the governor of Farringdon castle to yield the place up. The governor declined, but Cromwell had, in this process, acquired the available heavy horses which Maurice required for moving the artillery. The final act was a fight against Lord Goring, who was making his way to Oxford with some 4,000 mounted men. They encountered each other at Radcot Bridge, on the Thames north of Faringdon, on 3 May. Outnumbered, the Parliamentary horse made for Newbury and Goring came into Oxford on the following Monday.

Fairfax's orders were to relieve Taunton, and he moved out of Reading, where he had been supplied, on 1 May. On 7 May he was in Blandford in Dorset and on the same day Charles I at last set out from Oxford. This news, and fresh orders, reached Fairfax two days later. The bulk of the New Model Army turned back, marching for Dorchester, and three regiments of foot and one of horse were all the relief Taunton was sent. The party was commanded by Colonel Weldon and was made up of Lloyd's, Ingoldsby's and Fortescue's regiments and Graves's horse, of which only the first two were New Model units. The size of the force cannot have been great as Ingoldsby's and Lloyd's together numbered only 156 men. Fairfax made his way back and received, on 17 May, orders to invest Oxford. He arrived at the city five days later.

THE ROYALISTS' OPENING MOVES

Wednesday May 7. His Majestie left Oxford, attended with Prince Rupert, Prince Maurice, Earl of Lindsey, Duke of Richmond and Earl of Northampton. His troope and the Queenes lay that night at Woodstock. Thursday May 8. This morning at one of the clock an alarme waked us, and at daybreake the King marched with his 4 pieces of cannon, 8 boates in carriages, &c. ... Neare Stow on the Would, we joined Prince Rupert's army of horse and foot, eighteen myles.

So wrote Symonds.

The council of war that then met decided to divide the force, Goring returning to Somerset and the king heading for Chester. Goring's 3,000 horse were to return if summoned. Off he went, arriving too late to prevent the Parliamentarian relief column reaching Taunton; all Goring could do then was to bottle them up in the place and hope to starve them out. A modest portion of the New Model Army was thus held in check by a significant number of Royalists – a poor bargain.

The king's army moved on to Evesham where it was joined by Lord Astley's foot, some 3,300 men, and Prince Rupert's Bluecoat Regiment of Foot, 500 strong, as well as Lundsford's Regiment (another 500) from Somerset, the King's Lifeguard (200), Lisle's Foot (500) and Bard's, which was 300 strong. The foot was numbered at 5,300 by Symonds and he reports Langdale's horse at 2,500 men. Sir Henry Bard's was the erstwhile garrison of Campden House which he had quit and burned, allegedly on the orders of Prince Rupert in order to deny its use to the enemy. The shocked commentators of the time, Henry Slingsby and Walker among them, remarked that the house had 'cost £30,000 the building' and that the destruction was needless.

The royal progress was not without harassment. On 7 May Major George Purefoy's Parliamentarian garrison at Compton Winyates beat up part of the column near Stow and took prisoners, among them Rupert's gunsmith, Maurice's surgeon, cook and farrier and four of Rupert's Lifeguard. The next day Cromwell's Ironsides attacked the column's rearguard at Burford as he and Major-General Richard Browne, with foot drawn from his Abingdon garrison, followed with about 7,000 men.

The next house to suffer destruction was Hawkesley Hall, Kings Norton, while the king rested at Droitwich. It, too, was burned down.

THE COMMITTEE OF BOTH KINGDOMS RESPONDS

As the Royalist army meandered onwards, the Committee of Both Kingdoms bustled into action. They sent orders to Lord Leven's Scottish

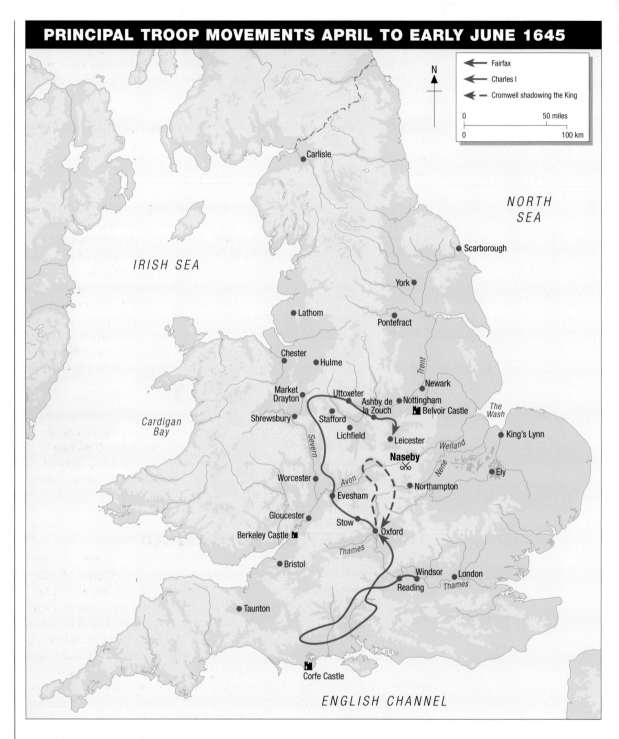

army to march, together with Lord Fairfax's men, to the support of Brereton outside Chester, and rendezvous at Barlow Moor, north of the Mersey. The Scots promptly went off in the direction of Carlisle, claiming that the roads were better that way and that the king had to be kept out of Scotland lest Montrose be reinforced. Brereton departed from Chester on 20 May. Sir Samuel Luke wrote to his father, Sir Oliver, three days later saying:

> *Sir W. Brereton's raising the siege without fighting has so disheartened the people that for the most part they resolve to take up arms no longer, but to yield themselves to the mercy of the strongest. Sir T. Fairfax's horse in Notts. have so discontented the country there that, as I hear, the greatest part of the gentry [are in] Newark...*

He went on to say that the Scots had similarly estranged the people of the North and that they were inclined to support the king. In short, the Parliamentarian control of the territory gained the previous year appeared to be in jeopardy. Correct or not, Sir Oliver no doubt spread the word in London.

Meanwhile, as Sir Thomas Fairfax left Newbury to invest Oxford, the Committee ordered Colonel Bartholemew Vermuyden to quit Cromwell and to ride into Yorkshire in order to link up with the Scots. The Royalists had only reached Market Drayton when Brereton abandoned the siege of Chester, and, unaware of the weakness related by Luke, they had already decided not to continue northwards but to move east towards Newark in order to approach Yorkshire from that secure place. The Committee halted Vermuyden, then recalled him and sent Cromwell off to East Anglia to raise more men; it appeared to those in London that the king had decided to attack the Eastern Association. On the other hand, Luke wrote to his father on 28 May suggesting an alternative plan:

> *...before this comes to your hands, his Majesty will be at Newark though Major Temple tell you he is before Leicester ... Massey has taken Evesham with some 300 men in it. Sir T. Fairfax lies before Oxford and the enemy shows no dislike of it, neither do I think he will these 2 months. By that time his Majesty may have done his pleasure in the North and then advanced southward into warmer air.*

THE QUESTION OF OXFORD

There was little sound reason for fearing for the safety of Oxford. First, Fairfax was too weak to seriously threaten the place and lacked artillery appropriate to a siege. Second, Colonel Legge had been assiduous in gathering in supplies, raising fortifications and opening up fields of fire for his guns, destroying houses in the suburbs where needful. However, this was the place where the families of those in the king's train had been left behind, and it was isolated not only by a blanket of rebels, but, as news that came on 28 May revealed, by the fact that the main line of communication through Evesham was falling into enemy hands. Sir John Culpepper, a Privy Councillor, wrote to Lord Digby on three successive days to plead for the relief of the city because of 'the temper of those within the town, the disaffection of the townsmen...' Sir Edward Walker observed that this 'staggered our Design, yet not so as instantly to return thither, or solely to abandon it; but only so retarded it, ... and also to act somewhat to divert Fairfax's Designs, by attempting the taking of Leicester, which was set of Foot as feasible.' This decision overtook the previous scheme of summoning Goring back from the West to the relief of Oxford.

The Royalists were then at Burton-on-Trent on their way to Ashby de la Zouche. Sir Henry Slingsby wrote, 'We march'd immediately away, till we came wth in 4 miles of Leister...' They arrived on 28 May and sent three bodies of inquisitive Parliamentarian horse briskly back into the town. The main Royalist force arrived the next day.

THE TAKING OF LEICESTER

Leicester was in part a town within medieval walls, with, in the south-west, a further enclave called the 'new work' or Newarke, an area enclosed by a wall in the 1350s and containing the castle and the hospital, but not directly connected with the town, for it lay outside the South Gate. The old fortifications had not been fully repaired nor had houses outside the walls been cleared, although it had been ordered on 19 April that 'the Grange howses & all buildings walls thereto belonginge & adioyninge lyinge neare the publicke worke on the South side of this towne shall be taken downe...' Major James Innes, who commanded a troop of dragoons in the town, later complained, 'they had left all places of advantage to the enemy undemolished...' Subsequently the committee responsible claimed that Colonel George Booth had advised, after visiting the town on 12 April, that 'The grand masters most sensible of danger, and careful of their own security, have all of them got houses in a place of the town called the Newarke, where they are fortifying themselves.' The townspeople, on the other hand, were left in fear of the enemy, and Booth evidently anticipated a backlash which would yield the town to the king.

There were outworks, earthen bastions on the south, east and north of Leicester, leaving the river to guard the west. On Thursday 29 May the eastern perimeter from St Margaret's Church to the East Gate, including the detached hornworks at Belgrave and Gallowtree gates, was under the command of Colonel Henry Grey and Lieutenant-Colonel Whitbroke. The southern part of the 3-mile defences was under the command of Sir Robert Pye and included Innes's dragoons.

That same day the Royalist army arrived to besiege Leicester. At this time the accepted conventions, if not exactly rules, of war regarding sieges provided for a number of 'summonses' to be made to the defenders to yield up the stronghold. The first was usually rejected, but if it was accepted the defenders were permitted to depart with all their weapons and supplies. If it was rejected the place would be blockaded, then the second summons would be made. Acceptance of that meant the supplies were forfeit, but the garrison could depart with its weapons. Rejection meant the bombardment could start and once a breach was made a third summons could be made which, if accepted, allowed the defenders to go, but weaponless, and civilians could depart with their possessions. If rejected, the soldiers might then withdraw to a castle or redoubt, yielding the town, but that might not be a practical proposition. In any event, a situation would eventually be reached in which the

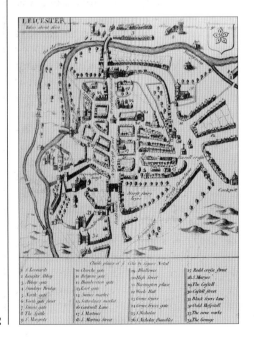

A map of Leicester dating from about 1600 showing the major features of the town before the defensive earthworks were raised. The river provided good protection in the west and north, so the principal assaults took place on the eastern and southern sides of town. (Beinecke Library, Yale University)

only course left to the attackers was to storm the defences, inevitably a costly business in terms of casualties. Bringing things to this pass exposed the defenders to extreme danger, for the frenzy of the action made the taking of prisoners or the respect of civilians impossible to expect – an outcome well known to, and understood by, all and amply demonstrated in the conflict in Europe in the immediate past.

Facing the southern outworks Rupert ordered the construction of a battery on the Rawdykes, a Roman aqueduct. Royalist troops got into some houses near St Sundays Bridge but were dislodged by a sally of dragoons under Innes. On Friday (30 May), Symonds records, 'His Highnes Prince Rupert sent a trumpet [a messenger under truce] (after he had shott two great pieces at the towne) to summon it for his Majestie, offering the burgesses and corporacion pardon, &c.' The messenger was detained. By early afternoon there were six guns in place on the old aqueduct, and out of the town came an envoy to ask permission to wait until the next day before giving a reply.

> *Then the Prince about three of the clock sent them an answer in lowder termes; six great peices from the fort on the south side of the towne playing on a stone wall unlined, and made ere six of the clock a breach of great space. Musketts and cannon continually putting us in mind of some thing done ... they in the towne had gotten up a handsome retrenchment with three flankers, (a great Spanish peice,) within four or five yards of the wall.*

Outside the North Gate Sir Bernard Astley's men were in position west and east of St Sundays Bridge and to their right, the east, was the earl of Northampton's horse, with Colonel Sir Henry Bard's foot facing the works outside Belgrave Gate. Opposite Horse Fair Leas and Gallowtree Gate on the south-east was Prince Rupert's Bluecoat Regiment of Foot and close to the battery facing the Newarke and up South Street were Colonel George Lisle's tertia and regiment, including the Shrewsbury Foot.

Within the Newarke work was proceeding feverishly on an earthen rampart and it was to complete this that the mayor tried to gain time by asking if they could reply to Rupert the next day. According to John Nichols in his *History of Leicestershire*, 'the women of the town wrought at it, although the cannon bullets and some splinters of stones fell amongst them, and hurt some of them; yet, to their exceeding commendation, they went on, and made it up...' As the Royal trumpeter who had carried the summons had been detained, Rupert kept the town trumpeter and sent in a drummer with a peremptory message demanding a reply within 15 minutes. It seems the conventional and courteous exchange of summons and reply had broken down and Rupert, impatient and insulted, opened fire.

Slingsby recorded: 'ye night was resolv'd upon to begin ye storm... The warning to be giv'n to fall on on every side was, upon ye shooting of six guns, & ye time to be about 12 o'Clock; every one had their places set, how one should second another, both horse & foot...' Symonds wrote, 'All the evening was a generall preparation to assaulte the towne, and a little before 12 of the clock in the night this violent storme began, and continued till after one.'

Lisle's men attacked the Newarke breach and came under a torrent of shot. Three assaults were thrown back. The cannon enfilading the line did much of the work and Colonel William St George, attempting to lead a charge on the gun, was 'shattered into small pieces' as were many others. So uncertain was the outcome that the king sent his Lifeguard of Foot forwards in support, though it emerged that they were not, in the event, required to conclude the matter. On the other side of town at Belgrave Gate, the one-armed Colonel Bard led his men in an attack with scaling ladders both on the main defences and on the hornworks. Nichols recounts that he was:

> beaten down by the butt-end of a musket ... and his major likewise stricken down by his side; some 16 of his men were slain upon the place, and 60 more mortally wounded out of 250 ... but setting upon it again, on a second attempt, with hand grenades thrown in amongst our men, entered within the works. Bard then broke down the drawbridge...

Farther towards the north Astley's men swarmed over the walls and opened the gates to admit the Northampton's horse. On the south-east Rupert's Bluecoats and his red-coated Firelocks also attacked and succeeded in planting his 'black colours on the battery within' as Symonds recounts. The fighting at the Newarke lasted longest, but eventually, surrounded as Royalists from the north and east joined the fight, resistance fragmented. A group of foot held out at the High Cross in the Market Place and a troop of Parliamentarian horse attempted a charge, but they were hugely outnumbered. The resistance by soldiers and civilians, including women, led inevitably to a sacking of the town. Richard Symonds's remarks are brief. 'In the meantime the foot gott in and fell to plunder, so that ere day fully open scarse a cottage unplundered. There were many Scots in this towne, and no quarter was given to any in the heat.'

The taking of Leicester had been an expensive business for both sides. Not only had the surviving attackers loaded themselves with plunder and left the place severely damaged, but they had lost, according to the *Moderate Intelligencer* of 14 June, about 400 killed. The defenders had lost some 300 and the Leicester Committee recorded that 719 bodies required burial. If a similar number were incapacitated for the time being by wounds, the depletion of the Royalist force was serious.

THE QUESTION OF OXFORD – AGAIN

The king wrote to the queen from Leicester Abbey on Saturday 31 May saying:

> My deare heart ... to tell thee of the good success which it hath pleased God to give me this day, of taking this town ... I am now hastening to the relief of Oxford, where, if it please God to bless me, according to these beginnings, it may make us see London next winter.

His hastening did not mean instant departure, for he remained until the following Wednesday, 4 June. In the meantime Lord Digby wrote on 3 June, with some sharpness, to Colonel Legge in Oxford, complaining that earlier letters to him and to Secretary Nicholas had not been answered. He continued:

> ...*nothing did ever import the Kings service more, than that wee should quickly, & positively know how long you can hold out. For if you can allow us but a month or six weeks time to pursuer our advantages whilst the enemy is engaged before that place. In my conscience, without hyperbole, you give the King his Crowne, & infallibly deliver the kingdome this summer for all its miseryes.*

He cited Montrose's victory around 16 May (meaning Auldearn, 9 May) as inflicting a loss of '3,000 killed dead' and having drawn away the Scots, thus giving the king the North for the asking. 'If wee be urg'd to attempt the succouring of you sooner (before Lo;Go; [Goring] & Charls Gerrett can come here to joyne, without us) in the action we shall ... loose all these other advantages...' But in Oxford panic prevailed and they replied that they could last a mere two weeks.

Sir Edward Walker held that the success at Leicester had been squandered: 'for instead of retiring towards Worcester to join with General Charles Gerrard ... or else marching Northward ... we turned our faces towards Oxford, which I must needs say was much against the Will of Prince Rupert.'

Not everyone followed. Symonds tells of Sir Richard Willys going back to Newark with 400 horse and that 'The Northern horse left his Majesties army, and notwithstanding his promise to them on the word of a King he would go into Yorkshire after Oxford was relieved; but upon persuasion returned and marched with us.' They were in Market Harborough on Thursday 5 June, and in the surrounding area. Symonds himself visited Desborough and Rushton to the south-east, for the Royalist forces were billeted in numerous villages around the town. The news that Fairfax had lifted the siege of Oxford and was marching towards Buckingham arrived the next day. 'This,' remarked Walker, 'was not welcome News, yet such as obliged us rather to make towards him and hazard a Battel, than to march Northwards and be met in the Face with the Scots, and have him in our Rear. From Harborow the Army marched to Daventry, and there stayed five Days, both to mark the Motion of Fairfax and to receive some Provision from Oxford.' Walker's recollection of the sequence of events and timing of decisions may be at fault, for most accounts say the army waited at Daventry while provisions were sent to Oxford.

PARLIAMENT RESPONDS: 2–13 JUNE

In the region between Leicester and the Eastern Association the Royalist success caused great alarm. Rockingham Castle became, with its 500-man garrison, the front line and its commander Sir John Norwich wrote on 2 June to Sir Samuel Luke in Newport Pagnell to report the Royalist pillaging of the countryside, but also to tell of the work of his men and the men from Burleigh and Kirby who, in small parties, 'had very good sport, brought in as many prisoners as our little garrison can well contain, some taken within 4 miles of Leicester ...'

On 2 June the Committee of Both Kingdoms sent orders to Fairfax to make preparations to move towards the Eastern Association and they also sent word to Cromwell to take three troops of horse to the Isle of Ely for the protection of the region. There was alarm in Northamptonshire and Buckinghamshire, voiced by Luke on 5 June when he wrote to the Committee about Royalist intentions, as he saw them. 'The report is that they intend to pass by Northampton and only face it and that this place is their aim ... we beg as speedy relief as may be.'

On 5 June the New Model Army marched away from Oxford, towards Marsh Gibbon, east of Bicester, and Fairfax deviated from the route to see how Sergeant-Major-General Skippon was faring in his assault on the Royalist outpost of Boarstall House which had been besieged since 23 May and where Joshua Sprigge noted that 'Though Granadoes ... did great execution, yet the Govern. held it out very resolutely ... the successe was not according to our desires (the Moat being much deeper than we expected.)' Luke reported to the earl of Essex that, also on Thursday 5 June, '200 of his Majesty's horse faced Northampton whereupon the troops there sallied out and gave them a repulse, took a captain and part of his troop.' On 7 June Sir John Norwich told Luke 'My scouts this morning brought me certain intelligence of the enemy's motion with his whole body and carriages towards Kelmarsh, being the way towards Northampton. Whither their design is I cannot conceive, whether for Northampton, Oxford or Banbury.' The confusion about the king's intentions only increased. Luke wrote to Lord Robartes on 6 June saying 'A country neighbour sent me word that the King's engineers with 100 horse were all yesterday upon Barnard's Green and Brackley, viewing the ground, which must be either for an entrenching or a fight.'

The Committee of Both Kingdoms was steadily assembling its assets on the Buckinghamshire border, between Newport Pagnell and Stoney Stratford. On Friday 6 June Fairfax reached Great Brickhill and moved on next day to Sherington, north-east of Newport. It was a position that kept the river, the great Ouse, between his army and that of the king and one which would allow Vermuyden, who reached Olney that evening, to join easily. A message was sent to ask Cromwell to come to them as well and on Sunday Fairfax called a council of war which resulted in a letter being sent to Parliament asking 'to give way he [Cromwell] might command their horse ... Which Letter was sent by Colonel Hammond, who went Post the same day to the Parliament, and was instantly returned with an answer according as we desired, to the great content of the General, and the whole Army.' That day also the true position became clear; the Royalist army was at Daventry and on Monday 9 June Colonel Nathaniel Whetham wrote to Luke from Northampton:

I am informed the Kings headqtrs to be at Davntry & intends to march this day, his horse had a rendezvous yesterday at Whilton where he drew 5 out of every Troope who marcht wth plundered Cattle to Oxford ... This night about the further end of Halston [Harlestone] Heath as wee conceive they made a great fyer ... some prisoners that wee bring in speak them to intend to joyne with Goring and then fight wth Sr Tho. Fairfax & if good success then for the North...

Philip Lea's improved 1680s version of Christopher Saxton's 16th-century map of Northamptonshire, showing roads for the first time. The main London to Holyhead road is marked with twin lines and the lesser roads emanating from Northampton to Market Harborough, Stoney Stratford and Coventry are shown with twin dotted lines. The single dotted lines are the administrative boundaries of the hundreds. Minor roads are not shown at all, but the river bridges from Saxton's map remain. In the Naseby campaign much of the movement was on minor roads. (Bodleian Library, Oxford, C17:46)

That same Monday, now assured that the king was not advancing in force on Northampton, Fairfax shifted his quarters to Stony Stratford. Luke said it was '… the bravest for bodies of men, horse and arms so far as the common soldiers as ever I saw in my life … the number is 8,000 foot and 5 or 6,000 horse.' Suddenly Colonel Vermuyden asked to be permitted to resign his commission, pleading business overseas, and Fairfax consented. The circumstances are unclear, and Luke thought that if he were offered promotion he might stay. He went on to say 'I hear several officers have petitioned the General that they might have liberty to leave the army, they being not able to live with that ungodly crew. They are grown so wild since they came near the enemy that our devout Christians cannot abide them.'

Wednesday 11 June was eventful. While Fairfax marched his army through the rain towards Northampton, where he halted at Wooton, just south of the town, the Royalists were probing down Watling Street. Luke told the earl of Essex that they had got as far as Towcester and into the Whittlewood Forest to the south.

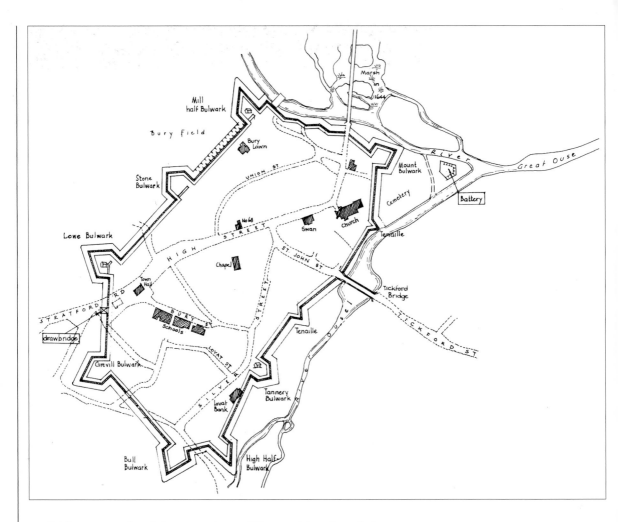

Map labels:
Marsh in 1644; Great Ouse; RIVER; River Ouse; Mill half Bulwark; Bury Field; Bury Lawn; Stone Bulwark; Mount Bulwark; Cemetery; Battery; UNION ST.; Lowe Bulwark; No 68; HIGH STREET; Swan; Church; Tenaille; Chapel; ST JOHN ST.; Tickford Bridge; TICKFORD ST.; Town Hall; STRATFORD RD.; BURY ST.; Schools; Tenaille; STREET; LOVAT ST.; drawbridge; Grevill Bulwark; Lovat Bank; LOVAT ST.; RIVER OUSEL; Tannery Bulwark; Bull Bulwark; High Half Bulwark

Sprigge remarks of the army that at Wooton 'they found there none of the best accommodation for quarter...' and 'The next day [Thursday 12 June], the Army marched to Guilsborough, (four miles on the west of Northampton, and within five miles of Borrough-hill, where the enemy still continued).' Perhaps it is wise to bear in mind that the statute mile of 1,760 yards was established in law only in 1593, and the 'customary mile' of 1.3 statute miles remained in common usage for many years which may explain the obvious inaccuracy of certain accounts. The next day Luke correctly names the place they moved to as Kislingbury, a village on the River Nene 3 miles west of Northampton, in a letter to Lord Essex, but later that same day he wrote another letter in which he says the king has gone from Daventry. Fairfax had patrols – 'commanded party of horse' is the phrase used by Sprigge – probing forwards towards Flore, Weedon Bec and Borough Hill. A few prisoners were taken, presumably from a standing patrol the Royalists had put on the route to Northampton, who revealed that Charles was out hunting at Fawsley. At about midnight Fairfax himself was out and three hours later saw for himself the shelters built by the Royalists going up in flames as the army moved off the hill. On his return to Kislingbury he was held up by having forgotten the password, and was made 'to stand in the wet, till [the sentry] sent for the Captain...' At about 5.00am his

A fortified frontier town, Newport Pagnell, commanded by Sir Samuel Luke, stood at the confluence of the rivers Ouse and Ousel. A plan is shown superimposed on a modern street layout. (Paul Woodfield)

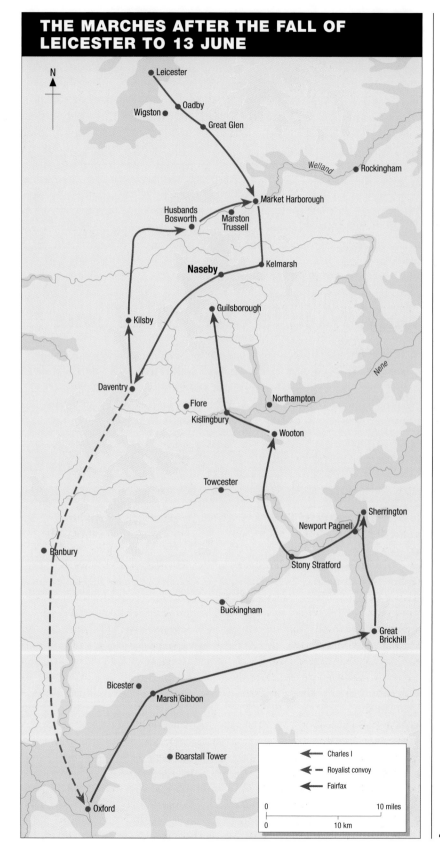

scoutmaster-general, Major Leonard Watson, confirmed that the king's men were on the move, and added the information that they had been surprised by the proximity of the Parliamentarian forces, a report probably inspired more by the wish of his spies to please their master than a true account of Prince Rupert's reactions.

A council of war was called for 6.00am and while it was in session Oliver Cromwell arrived with 600 horse and dragoons. 'Instantly orders were given for Drums to beat, Trumpets to sound to horse, and all our army to draw to a rendezvous...' Nathaniel Whetham reported that the rendezvous was in 'Harpole fields', presumably the common which appears in Thomas Eyre's map of 1790. From Fleetwood's Regiment Major Thomas Harrison was sent with a party of horse towards Daventry to monitor the Royalist march and Colonel Henry Ireton was ordered to march on the enemy's eastern flank as the northward march progressed, ready to seize the opportunity to attack should it present itself. The main body of the army was to make for Market Harborough and the headquarters that night was at Guilsborough.

THE ROYALISTS' WEEK: 7–13 JUNE

'Satterday, June 7, 1645. His Majestie marched to Daventree...' wrote Symonds, 'The army of foot lay in the field. His horse guards went to quarters at Staverton, one myle distant [2 miles to the west, in fact]...'

The purpose of the move, as Whetham had reported to Luke, was to convoy cattle and other provisions looted from Leicestershire and Northamptonshire down to Oxford. However, on Sunday Rupert wrote

The country west and immediately north of Northampton, mapped by Thomas Eyre and published, revised, in 1791, before canal building and road improvements created today's landscape. Daventry is upper left and the course of the River Nene can be traced to Northampton, passing by Flore (Flower) and Kislingbury, north of which is Harpole Common and Althorp, the seat of the Spencers. (Northamptonshire Record Office, 1298)

from Daventry to William Legge saying 'There was a plot to send the King to Oxford, but it is undone. The Chief of this counsel was the feare somm menn had that the souldiers should take from them, the influence which now they poses [possess] with the King.' He also expresses the desire to meet with Legge, but cannot seek leave of absence to do so 'for fear of the rest of the Officers.' The letter was signed '198' which was Rupert's usual cypher for his name. The communication gives some idea of how insecure Rupert felt and of the uncertainty at the very summit of the Royalist command structure.

In the meantime precise information about the movements of Fairfax's army appears to have been scarce. On Tuesday 10 June, Symonds reports, an envoy visited the Royalist headquarters. He says, 'A trumpet came from Fairfax for exchange of prisoners from Newport Paganell.' On Wednesday there were clashes on either side of Towcester, suggesting that the Royalist interest was in the protection of the Daventry–Banbury–Oxford route with an eastern flank along Watling Street, which was a rational decision for a force planning to depart for Newark as soon as Oxford had been reprovisioned. The Parliamentarian move towards Northampton, a mere 10 miles from Borough Hill, was only understood on Thursday, when a small skirmish, possibly near Flore, raised the alarm. The army was brought together on Borough Hill, the hill fort immediately east of Daventry where the infantry had been sheltering in temporary huts, and, in the early hours of Friday 13 June, moved off.

That they were doing so was known at once; Fairfax himself observed the fires from the burning huts on the hill. Sir Edward Walker declares that the intention was to make for Newark by way of Melton Mowbray,

The earliest known painting of the battle of Naseby created c.1680 by an unknown artist and clearly derived from the Streeter illustration on page 63.

A photograph of Naseby in 1855, when the surviving cob-built, thatched houses gave an appearance probably very similar to that of the village of 1645. (Westaway Collection)

Market Harborough being the first stop. As the Parliamentarian army was evidently very close, the route by which they had come, through Kelmarsh, Naseby and Cold Ashby, was closed to them. The wagons had to make for Kilsby and the bridge over the River Avon at Catthorpe while the horse could take a short cut from Ashby St Ledgers to Crick and Stanford on Avon, where Charles I dined with Sir Thomas Cave, before joining the main road to Harborough through Husbands Bosworth. Attempts were made to confuse the enemy. Some, including horse and artillery, set out along the Southam road westwards at least as far as Shuckburgh, as if making for Warwick, before turning north and Whetham wrote, 'One thing observable 2 [men] that came from the Kings Army this morning [13 June] when they were upon their march say that 7 horse Collors [colours] were sett upon Baggage Waggons and marcht as a Regimt of horse, besides a 1000 weemen and 500 boyes at least.' This appears to be an attempt to suggest they were in greater strength than they actually were.

The presence of the enemy was clear to Slingsby: 'In our march we understood yt General Fairfax follow'd wth his army upon ye side of us 6 miles distant. Wn we took our Quarters, we made ye head Quarters at Harborrow; our horse lay Quarter'd in Villages between us & ye enemy...' The king slept at Lubenham that night, his troop of horse and perhaps part of the baggage train at Theddingworth, both on the road west of the town. A troop of cavalry, said to be of Rupert's Lifeguard, was as far south of this line as the village of Naseby, and there Ireton's men found them: some, it is said, playing quoits, others sitting at a long oak table taking supper. While a few Royalists were taken prisoner, both sides hastened away to report the incident.

Slingsby gives a different account. '...[the enemy] gave [us] an Alarum, but presently were encounter'd wth a party of our horse, & chas'd until they came to see where they had made their fire, in an open field' so it is clear that Langdale's Northern Horse was also out scouting that evening. Contact had been made.

THE BATTLE OF NASEBY

BATTLE PLANS AND THE START OF THE DAY

The news of the Royalist presence was received in the Parliamentarian command with satisfaction and a determination to pursue and, if possible, to bring them to battle. To the north, Charles was aroused from his bed and a hasty council of war was convened in Market Harborough. Sir Edward Walker recorded the events:

> But that Night an Allarum was given, that Fairfax with his army was quartered within six miles of us. This altered our design, and a Council being presently called, resolutions were taken out to fight; and rather to march back and seek him out, than to be sought or pursued, contrary (as 'tis said) to Prince Rupert's Opinion; it being our unhappiness, that the Faction of the Court, whereof the most powerful were the Lord Digby and Mr John Ashburnham, and that of the Army ever opposed and were jealous of others.

Doubt has been cast on the accuracy of this report, suggesting that the council (which Walker evidently did not attend, for he says ''tis said') never took place. Digby is cited in support of this proposal, despite his interest in being absolved from involvement in such a conference, and a meeting between the king and Rupert is suggested. However, nobody disputes that Rupert wished to march north, and that someone, the king alone or with others, ruled otherwise. That the Royalists expected reinforcements is unlikely, for on Monday 9 June Symonds had recorded news of Goring's fight at Taunton so that hoping for his presence in Leicestershire by the end of the week was clearly out of the question. On 10 June one of Prince Charles's council wrote to Digby to argue that the conquest of Taunton should have priority, and it is certain that the letter arrived and therefore Goring was not expected. Rupert would be obliged to face Fairfax here, with the Oxford Army alone.

Symonds recorded:

> Satterday we marched out of our quarters about two of the clock in the morning, and intelligence was that the enemy was very neare, and had beat up some quarters, at least given an alarme. A generall rendesvous of all his Majesties army this morning at Haverburgh at seven of the clock...

The army climbed the hills to the south, past East Farndon and on 'a Hill whereupon a Chappell stood' as its church was styled in Slingsby's account, drew up, ready for action. Sir Edward described it as 'upon rising Ground of very great Advantage about a mile from Harborow, which we left on our Back, and there put in order and disposed to give or receive the Charge.' There can be little doubt that this position is astride the East Farndon to Clipston road, with the left flank secured on the old parish boundary hedge of Little Oxendon and the right by the steeply sloping hill that topples from the church into the Welland Valley. To the rear the land also falls away steeply and the position has all the advantages of a motte: a fine place to defend but with no scope for manoeuvre or orderly retreat. And there, from about 8.00am, the Royalists waited, peering southwards towards the ridge of hills north of Naseby village along which the road runs that they had taken from Kelmarsh only a week earlier, for a sign of the enemy.

THE NEW MODEL ADVANCES

The Parliamentarian army had quartered itself around Guilsborough, billeted in neighbouring villages and encamped in the soggy fields. With news of the proximity of the king's forces, Sprigge records:

> The General with the Army advanced by three of the clock in the morning, from Gilling [Guilsborough] towards Naseby, with an intention to follow close upon the Enemy, and (if possible) retard their march with our Horse, till our foot could draw up to them, in case they should have marched on to Leicester... By five in the morning, the Army was at Rendezvouz near Naseby, where his Excellency received intelligence by our Spies, that the Enemy was at Harborough; with this further, that it was still doubtfull, whether he meant to march away, or to stand us.

The heights upon which Naseby stands put the village and its windmill in clear view from the south. The roads approach from the direction of Thornby and Guilsborough, once the little stream north of Guilsborough has been crossed, up long ridges, and the Thornby route was certainly passable by wheeled traffic of the time. Baggage and artillery trains would keep to the roads, infantry would be more flexible and cavalry could largely please themselves. The vital requirement was to meet at the desired place and a clear rendezvous landmark was needed. Naseby windmill, the site of which is today crowned with the Obelisk monument, served the purpose.

Naseby windmill stood on a level plain sloping slightly north to south with its northern horizon 800 yards away where the land drops sharply to the rippled valley floor before rising to East Farndon, 4 miles away. The ridge at Naseby where the road turns east for Kelmarsh is 632ft above sea level while that at East Farndon, to the rear of the Royalists' position, stands at 518ft. Fairfax's army was out of Rupert's sight, and vice versa. The road to Market Harborough for wheeled vehicles lay through Kelmarsh, for the precipitate escarpment to be negotiated on the Clipston route limited it to foot traffic. The 1630 map of Naseby parish shows no road for Clipston, and the route past the windmill is marked 'Kelmarsh way' and along that road the commanders rode forwards to see what they could see. From the edge of the ridge-top the view of the Royalist array across the valley was uninterrupted.

Naseby church spire rises beyond the ridge north of the village. The hillside is steep and one or two of the many gullies that cut into the slope can be seen, now filled with trees. A virtually unassailable position. (John Kliene)

'Great bodies of the Enemies horse were discerned on the top of the hill this side of Harborough,' Sprigge wrote, 'which increasing more and more in our view, begat a confidence in the General ... that he meant not to draw away, as some imagined, but that he was putting his Army in order, either there to receive us, or to come to us...' Orders were given to Skippon to prepare for battle. Meanwhile Fairfax and Cromwell examined the terrain immediately to their front and could not, given that they desired to tempt the enemy to fight, have been pleased with what they saw. The steep hillsides were uncultivated and cut with little gullies where the rain drained off the ridge, nurturing growth of furze (gorse) on the hillside and feeding the boggy ground below. A pamphlet published in 1647, *A Just Apology for an Abused Army,* offers an account of what happened next:

> *Cromwell, who as though he had received direction from God himselfe, where to pitch the Battell; did advise ... saying, 'Let us I beseech you draw back to yonder hill, which will encourage the enemy to charge us, which they cannot doe in that place, without their absolute ruine.' This he spake with so much cheerful resolution and confidence, as though he had forseen the victory, and was therefore condescended to...*

From the turning in the road there is today a good view west and in the treeless landscape of the time an excellent view could be had of the shallow valley of Broadmoor and the hill to the south, 'yonder hill', while 'that place' falls away to the north from where they stood. The decision to move was made.

THE MOVE TO DUST HILL

On the far side of the valley things were not so clear. It might have been that Rupert and his officers had a glimpse of the enemy horse on the forward edge of the ridge, for Slingsby says 'we could diserne ye enemy's horse upon another Hill about a Mile or two before us...' Walker makes no such mention, but says it was necessary to verify intelligence reports of the enemy's presence, and that for that purpose the scoutmaster,

From a point close to that from which Fairfax and Cromwell viewed the scene looking north-west, the modern Dust Hill Farm is on the right, the pale fields of Broadmoor are in the centre and left in the distance, and the ploughed curve of Lodge Hill is in the centre. The steepness of the ridge is indicated by the tops of trees emerging from the gullies on the hillside.

Francis Ruce, was sent forwards. Given the lie of the land, it is clear that the only way Ruce could locate the Parliamentarian army was to scale the slope that Cromwell called 'that place', at which point he would have been in amongst his adversaries. Maybe he should have done so, but the accusation made by Walker of his returning 'with a Lye in his Mouth' is misplaced, for he reported 'that he had been two or three Miles forward, and could neither discover or hear of the Rebels.' If he went no farther than he said he was telling the truth, even if he was a poor and timorous scout.

Rupert decided to look for himself and took a party of horse forward. Slingsby, who was with the Northern Horse on the left wing and probably had limited knowledge of what was being done by Rupert on the right, wrote as though he was riding with him:

> ...prince Ruport draws forth a good body of horse, & advanceth towards ye enemy, where he sees their horse marching up upon ye side of ye Hill to yt place where after they embattl'd their whole army: but being hindred of any nearer approach, by reason ye place between us & ym, was full of burts [Bur-reed, sparganium?] & Water, we wheel'd about, & by our guides were brought upon a fair peice of ground, partly corn & partly heath, under Naseby, about half a mile distant from ye place.

From this it seems that the New Model Army, with Ireton's horse in the van, were moving in battalia towards Mill Hill while the scouting party had found the boggy area at the foot of the slope. It was entirely impractical to withdraw at this stage; the only course was to move west as well and call for the king to move. 'The prince having taken his ground began to put in order horse in sight of ye enemy ... immediately he sends to ye King, to hasten away ye foot, & Cannon, wch were not yet come off ye Hill whre they first made ye randevous...'

While the New Model Army had a fairly simple stroll across the hilltop towards their new position, the Royalists had to come south before wheeling west to make for the flag placed on Moot Hill to show the line of march. Meanwhile the wheeled traffic, the artillery and baggage trains, had to make their way along two sides of the triangle, down the hill to Clipston and then turning right to climb towards Sibbertoft along the narrow road between the two closes of Nobold.

THE GROUND AND THE BATTALIA

The ground on which the opposing sides stood was limited on each flank. On the west was the parish of Sulby. The parish boundary hedge is at right angles to the Naseby–Sibbertoft boundary, which runs west to east across Broadmoor, and extends about 930 yards south and 630 yards north of it to a point at which it turns west. A stock-proof barrier, it formed a solid obstacle to troops and animals, although not, of course, to musket fire. Access to the southern end was by a lane from the south-west. On the east the stream which runs across Broadmoor on the Naseby–Sibbertoft boundary passes through the hedge, nourishing marshy ground. On the other side of Broadmoor a smaller stream runs round the north flank of Lodge Hill, on which the Naseby parish map of 1630 depicts the warrener's house or lodge, and is joined by another stream originating in the little valley to the south, to supply the boggy area below the ridge from which Fairfax evaluated the terrain. Broadmoor itself is fairly level, and the streams draining it east and west would create marshy conditions. The warrener had been the custodian of the rabbit warren and the hill on which he lived, now Lodge Hill, is sandy and suitable for burrows even today. In the 17th century the hill would have been a considerable obstacle to the free movement of horse because of the danger of breaking their legs. The frontage available for Fairfax's battalia south of Broadmoor was therefore limited by Sulby Hedges on the west and the boggy ground east of Lodge Hill, while Lodge Hill itself was a hazard over which cavalry had to pick its way. North of Broadmoor the corner of Sulby Hedges similarly imposed the western limit and the eastern end of Dust Hill defined the other end of the ground upon which the Royalists could form.

The numbers of Parliamentarian troops have, in the past, been consistently overstated in light of the figures in the State Papers. The frontage occupied by the foot was laid down by the drill-books as 3ft per man in 'order' 1½ft in 'close order' to which some commentators have added another 1½ft to represent a person, which is not what the books actually say. In fact, 3ft is the distance elbow to elbow when a man stands 'arms set a-kimbow' and a shoulder-to-shoulder 'close order' stance does occupy 1½ft. The former was mandated for musketeers, and the latter for pike 'when that are to receive a Charge from the horse: that they may stand the stronger, by so much as they are the closer serried together...' according to Barriffe, who goes on, 'as also for the ranks of Muskittiers, when they are to poure on a salute of shot.' Taking 3ft per man cannot, therefore, be far off the truth. For horse in fighting formation, thigh to thigh, 5ft emerges from similar study. From the battle plans and Streeter's pictogram the front line regiments can be identified and the figures for their front lines, assuming foot are six deep and horse three deep, come to about 800 foot and 500 horse and thus frontages of 800 yards and 833 yards respectively. To this, in ideal conditions, spaces between the regiments, troops or battalia have to be added. The distance from Sulby Hedges to the eastern side of Lodge Hill is about 2,000 yards, which leaves little room for

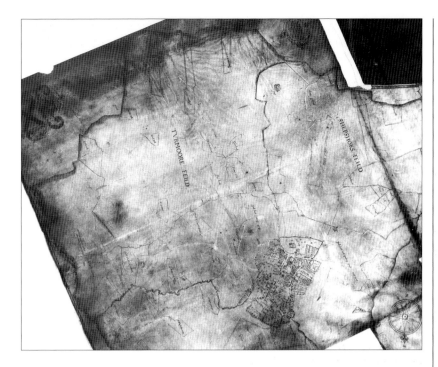

The Naseby parish map of 1630 naturally stops at the Sibbertoft boundary on the north and the Sulby boundary on the west, where the line of the curved access lane is shown. Warren House is shown top right, in the centre of the rabbit warren on what is now called Lodge Hill. The land holdings marked may not have been physically enclosed at the time, or, if they were, only with dry-hedging, fencing made with hedge off-cuts that were easily flattened. (Suffolk Record Office, HB56: 2803)

inter-formation interval spaces, but the frequently made suggestion that the front line is massively overmanned is unsustainable. However, men accustomed to parade-ground formations would certainly find that they had to make adjustments in such circumstances, and from the records of the time it appears that this is exactly what took place. As to the Royalist forces, with fewer men, it is evident that a front of similar width would be satisfactory.

Before the order to move was given, the New Model Army had been drawn up just outside Naseby in battle formation: Ireton's horse on the left, the foot in the centre and Cromwell's horse on the right of the line. A left turn and they were ready to march off towards the Closter Hill ridge and thus as they arrived Ireton formed his horse in the traditional manner, the foot did the same under Skippon's eye and Cromwell's horse found themselves with insufficient room. Fortunately the Royalist army had farther to move and was not ready to attack, and so there was time to re-organize. Sprigge records:

> But considering it might be of advantage to us to draw up our Army out of sight of the Enemy; who marched upon a plain ground towards us: we retreated about an 100 paces from the ledge of the Hill, that so the Enemy might not perceive in what form our battell was drawn, nor see any confusion therein...

Skippon, it was said, became annoyed by what he took to be an unnecessary manoeuvre, but as he was positioned on the left of the foot he lacked the opportunity to appreciate the problem fully. As it was, only the two regiments of horse on the left of Cromwell's front, Whalley's and Pye's, had clear ground before them and even then Pye's drew up half in the front line and half in the second, while Cromwell's was faced with Lodge Hill and Rossiter's, a late arrival, and Fiennes's were squashed in

THE BATTLE AREA, WITH TROOP MOVEMENTS UP TO THE START OF THE FIGHT

The Royalists took up a position between East Farndon and Little Oxendon early in the morning, from which they could not see the flat fields around Naseby windmill, where the Parliamentarian Army made its rendezvous. From the escarpment north of the windmill Fairfax and Cromwell had a good view and decided to move north-west. Seeing this, Rupert ordered a matching move.

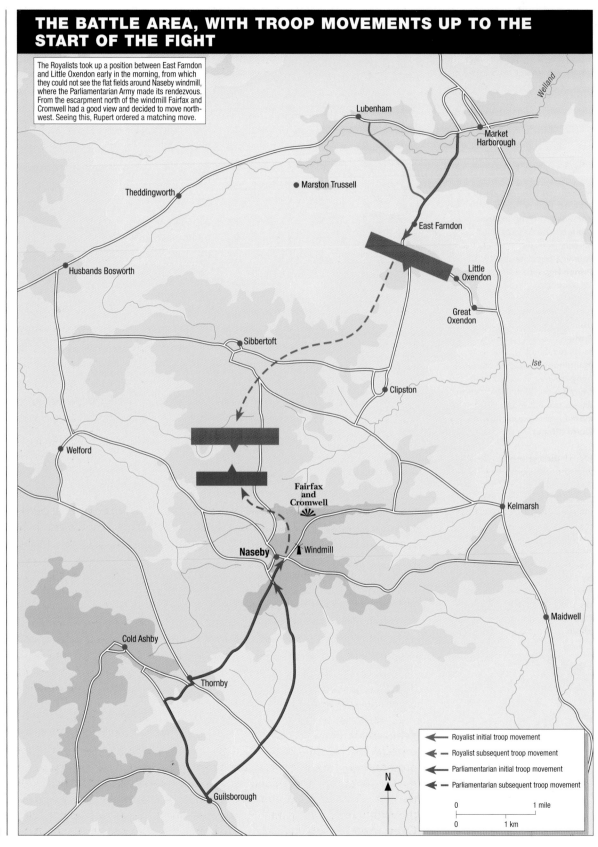

Welland

Lubenham

Market Harborough

Marston Trussell

Theddingworth

East Farndon

Husbands Bosworth

Little Oxendon

Great Oxendon

Sibbertoft

Ise

Clipston

Welford

Fairfax and Cromwell

Kelmarsh

Naseby

Windmill

Maidwell

Cold Ashby

Thornby

Royalist initial troop movement

Royalist subsequent troop movement

Parliamentarian initial troop movement

Parliamentarian subsequent troop movement

N

0   1 mile

0   1 km

Guilsborough

ABOVE **From behind Sulby Hedges, centre, Longhold Spinney is in the distance on the left. The Royalist line ran on an axis from the right of the spinney, past the buildings of Prince Rupert's Farm towards the tree in the hedge on the left. In the far distance on the right a ploughed field marks the slope from Broadmoor up towards the Parliamentary line and the field to its left has the Cromwell Monument against its upper hedgerow. In the near field, Okey's men fell back to the right where the dip in the hedge-line marks a change in ground level. (John Kliene)**

RIGHT **Sulby Hedges run south with the dragoons' position along the curving hedge to the right. Straight ahead is the line of charge of Maurice's horse, left of the point on the horizon to which the hedge-line goes. Above and right of the farm building in the distance is the hill occupied by Skippon's regiment, with Ireton to the right. To the left in the distance is the ploughed field shown in the panoramic photograph above. (John Kliene)**

behind. The front line of foot from right to left, with numbers given from the State Papers, was: Fairfax's (1,397), Montagu's (1,025), Pickering's (1,126), Waller's (560) and Skippon's (1,533) and from their number a forlorn hope of some 300 muskets was sent forwards. On the left Ireton's, Vermuyden's and Butler's formed the front line of horse. Cromwell had obtained Fairfax's consent to appoint a second in command of the horse to take charge of the left wing, and so Henry Ireton became Commissary-General of Horse.

Across the valley on Dust Hill the Royalist forces, which had marched in battalia from East Farndon, assembled on a line about 1,500 yards distant on the west and 800 yards on the eastern flank of the battlefield. Facing Ireton was Prince Maurice's wing of horse near the corner of Sulby Hedges, with three tertia of foot in the centre and Sir Marmaduke Langdale's horse on the east, the Royalist left, facing Cromwell's.

One crucial modification was made to the Parliamentarian deployment before the battle began. Probably from the right rear on Mill Hill, Cromwell scanned the field and grasped the advantage presented by the secure barrier of Sulby Hedges. Looking west, he could see the dragoons close by the ammunition train which had made use of the road leaving Naseby on the north-west, leaving the baggage near the windmill, to move to the Parliamentarian left rear. Colonel John Okey wrote, 'I was half a mile behinde in a Medow giving my men

Ammunition, and had not the Lieutenant Gen. come presently, & caused me with all speed to mount my men, & flank our left Wing, which was the King's right Wing of horse...' Here Okey's text rushes into an account of the attack without pause and his story, like so many others upon which we depend, makes no reference to the lapse of time between separate incidents and must be treated with care.

THE BATTLE BEGINS

Okey obeyed Cromwell's order with enthusiasm, moving quickly into the open grazing land west of the Sulby Hedges by way of the access lane at the south-eastern corner. The security of the hedge-line emboldened them to charge forwards, down the hillside and up the gentle slope beyond. They would have been clearly visible to the cavalry on Dust Hill and the musketeers with Maurice's horse made ready for them. Okey reported:

> ...by the time I could get my men to [a]light, and deliver up their Horses, in a little close, the Enemy drew towards us: which my men perceiving, they with shooting and rejoicing received them, although they were incompassed on the one side with the King's Horse, and on the other side with Foot and Horse to get the Close...

To what extent the Royalist horse could get at the dragoons is unknown, but clearly the hedge was no defence against a musket and the detected shotfall suggests that incoming fire forced Okey back from the flat top of the hill down the slope to a more sheltered position from which his men laid down heavy fire on Maurice's horse. Slingsby wrote, 'they had possess'd an Hedge upon our right wing wch they had lin'd wth Musqueteers to Gall our horse, (as indeed they did) before we could come up to charge theirs.' John Rushworth, secretary to Fairfax, recorded, 'our Dragoones begun the Battaile Flanking the right wing of the Enemies Horse as they charged...' There is no evidence that at this

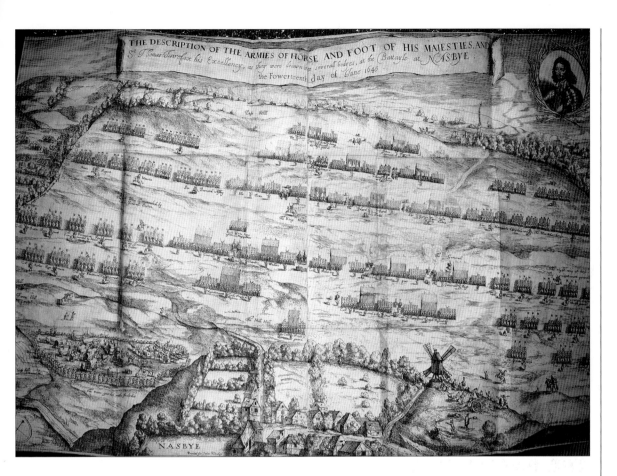

THE DESCRIPTION OF THE ARMIES OF HORSE AND FOOT OF HIS MAJESTIES, AND Sr Thomas Fairefaxe his Excellency, as they were drawn into severall bodyes, at the Battayle at NASBYE the Fowerteenth day of June 1645

NASBYE

Streeter's 'Description' of the armies at Naseby, folded out from the copy of Sprigge into which it was bound for publication in 1647. It is a conventional representation of the period, in which the armies fill the entire width of the page regardless of scale and on which the forces are shown in standard numbers and formations. It must therefore be interpreted with care. (Naseby Battlefield Project)

moment Rupert was anywhere other than his appropriate position: with the king and his staff and reserves. The outbreak of fire on his right was unexpected and he would naturally ride across, a move that needed only a couple of minutes, to appraise himself of the cause. It was clear that the right wing of Royalist horse was unable to stand under this fire and so moved forwards, Rupert with them. As Slingsby continues, 'It fell upon Prince Ruport to charge at ye disadvantage, & many of ye Regiment wound'd by shot from ye hedge before we could joyne wth theirs on yt wing: but so behav'd himself in ye charge, yt he beat ym up upon yt wing beyond ye Hills...'

Sprigge remarks, 'Upon the approach of the Enemies [Royalist] Right wing of Horse, our Left wing drawing down the brow of the hill to meet them, the Enemy coming on fast, suddenly made a stand...' The pause puzzled Ireton's men and they, too, stood. An explanation that the ground was broken up by 'pits of water, and other pieces of ditches...' is offered but also it seems that the unplanned move by Maurice was precipitated by Okey's fire and, having for the moment escaped it, the Royalist horse settled back into formation before riding on to meet the advancing Parliamentarian troopers. An arc of shot lies across Broadmoor emanating from the probable position of the dragoons.

The initial Royalist charge was successful only in part. Rupert's journal states briefly, 'and the right wing, which P[rince] Maurice commanded, P[rince] R[upert] was there and beat back the right wing of their horse and a great part of their foot.' It was rather more complicated than that.

63

THE ROYALIST ATTACK

A view from the west over the open fields of Naseby and Sibbertoft parishes, where the battle began at about 10.00am on Saturday 14 June 1645. In the first phase the Royalists came close to breaking their adversaries, but the stubborn resistance of the Parliamentarian foot and the success of their right wing of horse turned the tide.

Note: Gridlines are shown at intervals of 1,000m/1,094yds

ROYALIST FORCES
(after Foard, from de Gomme)

The Right Wing of Horse
A   Prince Rupert's and Prince Maurice's Lifeguards.
B   Prince Rupert's Regiment
C   The Queen's and Prince Maurice's Regiments
D   The Earl of Northampton's Regiment
E   Sir William Vaughan's Regiment

The Foot
Sir Bernard Astley's Tertia of Foot
F   The Duke of York's Regiment
G   Sir Edward Hopton's Regiment
H   Sir Richard Page's Regiment

Bard's Tertia
I   Sir Henry Bard's Regiment and the Queen's Lifeguard
J   Sir John Owen's and Col Radcliffe Gerard's Regiments

Sir George Lisle's Tertia
K   Sir George Lisle's and Col St George's Regiments
L   The Shrewsbury Foot (Broughton's, Tillier's, Hunks's, Warren's and Gibson's Regiments)

Three Divisions of Horse
M, N   Bagot's and Leveson's
O   Col Thomas Howard's

The Left Wing of Horse
P, Q, R   The Northern Horse, three divisions under Sir Marmaduke Langdale
S   Sir Horatio Carey's Regiment
T   Northern Horse, one division under Sir William Balckiston

The Reserve
U, V   The Newark Horse
W   The Lifeguard of Foot
X   The King's Lifeguard of Horse
Y   Prince Rupert's Bluecoat Regiment of Foot

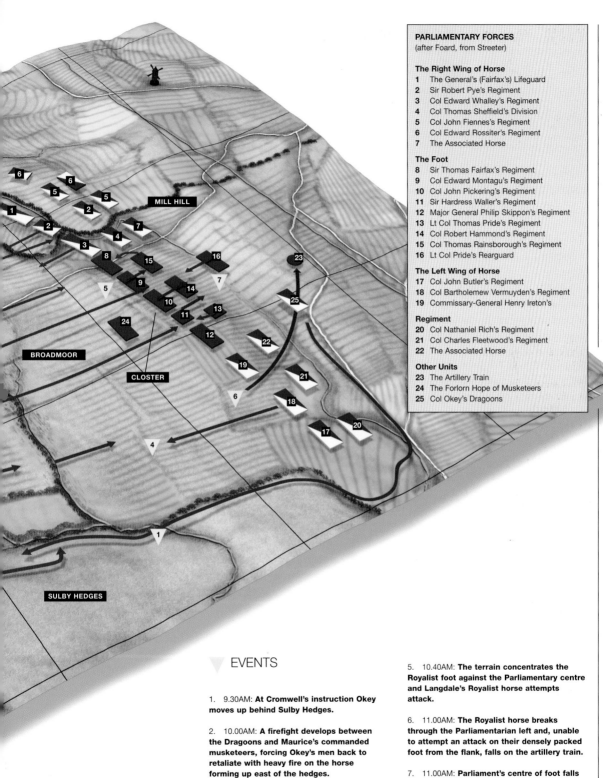

MILL HILL

BROADMOOR

CLOSTER

SULBY HEDGES

PARLIAMENTARY FORCES
(after Foard, from Streeter)

The Right Wing of Horse
1   The General's (Fairfax's) Lifeguard
2   Sir Robert Pye's Regiment
3   Col Edward Whalley's Regiment
4   Col Thomas Sheffield's Division
5   Col John Fiennes's Regiment
6   Col Edward Rossiter's Regiment
7   The Associated Horse

The Foot
8   Sir Thomas Fairfax's Regiment
9   Col Edward Montagu's Regiment
10 Col John Pickering's Regiment
11 Sir Hardress Waller's Regiment
12 Major General Philip Skippon's Regiment
13 Lt Col Thomas Pride's Regiment
14 Col Robert Hammond's Regiment
15 Col Thomas Rainsborough's Regiment
16 Lt Col Pride's Rearguard

The Left Wing of Horse
17 Col John Butler's Regiment
18 Col Bartholemew Vermuyden's Regiment
19 Commissary-General Henry Ireton's

Regiment
20 Col Nathaniel Rich's Regiment
21 Col Charles Fleetwood's Regiment
22 The Associated Horse

Other Units
23 The Artillery Train
24 The Forlorn Hope of Musketeers
25 Col Okey's Dragoons

▼ EVENTS

1.   9.30AM: **At Cromwell's instruction Okey moves up behind Sulby Hedges.**

2.   10.00AM: **A firefight develops between the Dragoons and Maurice's commanded musketeers, forcing Okey's men back to retaliate with heavy fire on the horse forming up east of the hedges.**

3.   10.15AM: **Unable to stand under the musket fire, the Royalist horse moves forwards.**

4.   10.25AM: **Maurice's and Ireton's opposing horse in action near Sulby Hedges.**

5.   10.40AM: **The terrain concentrates the Royalist foot against the Parliamentary centre and Langdale's Royalist horse attempts attack.**

6.   11.00AM: **The Royalist horse breaks through the Parliamentarian left and, unable to attempt an attack on their densely packed foot from the flank, falls on the artillery train.**

7.   11.00AM: **Parliament's centre of foot falls back on its reserves and the Royalist second line advances.**

8.   11.30AM: **The Parliamentary reserves force the Royalist centre to waver as Langdale's horse is repulsed by the left of Cromwell's front line.**

The opposing horse met at the bottom of the northern slope of Sulby Hill, where the ground gave way to Sprigge's 'pits of water, and other pieces of ditches which they expected not...' each having charged. On the extreme left of Ireton's force the two divisions of Colonel John Butler's Regiment, slow off the mark, were hard hit and Butler himself was seriously wounded. To their right, one division of Vermuyden's and both of Ireton's were more effective, and Sprigge told how 'coming to a close Charge, routed the two opposite Divisions of the Enemy' and in the confusion a third was 'carried away in the disorder of the other two.' Thus, while the flank adjacent to Sulby Hedges had been opened to the Royalists, they had themselves been thrown back from the Parliamentarian infantry's flank. Here Ireton, apparently under the impression that the cavalry action was all but over on his side of the field, turned to assault the Duke of York's Regiment of Foot which was pressing Skippon's men severely. It proved to be an error, for the foot stood, Ireton had his horse shot under him, a pike wound in the thigh and a halberd cut to his face before he was obliged to surrender. Meanwhile the Royalist reserves of horse, and doubtless the reformed survivors of the earlier setback, were coming on. Okey claimed that it was only the musket fire of his men on Northampton's flank that saved Butler's from total annihilation, but the charge smashed through Fleetwood's and the remains of the Parliamentarian left and reserves fled. The mass of Maurice's command pursued. Colonel Sir William Vaughan appears to have intended to wheel left, but found the valley to the rear of Skippon's front thronged with men presenting an impenetrable obstacle. His intention frustrated, he pressed straight on. Rupert, according to his journal, then returned to the king and to his own regiment of foot while the cavalry engagement continued. Rushworth wrote, 'A party of theirs that broke through the left wing of Horse, came quite behind the rear to our traine, the leader of them being a person somewhat in habit like the Generall, in a red Mountero...' Mistaking this person for one of their own, the commander of the guard of firelocks asked him how the day went, to which his visitor replied inviting his surrender: 'they cryed no, Gave fire and instantly beat them off...' Rushworth says they later learned the man in the red cap was Rupert, an attractive but unlikely and uncorroborated identification which has taken firm root in folklore.

The Royalist infantry, deprived of their flanking cavalry by the premature advance caused by Okey, started forwards, the right of the line, moving first so that the line as a whole wheeled, compensating for the greater distance they had to cover to reach their enemies. The effect of the

Edward Fitzgerald illustrated his letters to Thomas Carlisle in the 1840s, only 20 years after the land had been enclosed. Its appearance without hedges is easily imagined. The road from Dust Hill to Naseby and its church is on the left, passing the green field that today has the Cromwell Monument on its far hedge-line. Skippon's men defended the height in front of the grave that Fitzgerald found. (Cambridge University Library Add.7062)

Looking east from Skippon's frontage with Longhold Spinney far left. The valley that cuts back into Closter Ridge, so difficult to identify from a distance, is clearly seen. This hedge-line passes south of the Cromwell Monument and has been planted north of the hilltop behind which Parliament's forces withdrew.

forlorn hope on their progress is not recorded, and it can be assumed that the little band discharged their firearms and missed before fleeing to shelter amongst their comrades. The ridge and furrow ran north to south across Turmoore Field and thus did not impede progress. The northern edge of Closter Hill drops quite steeply from a shallowly domed top, and its frontage is not a simple, uniform slope. In the centre a shallow valley, a re-entrant in technical terms, cuts back into the hill. It is only some 15ft deep, but that is more than twice the height of a man and the difference in the slope an advancing line experiences will have its effect. Those in the centre, at the foot of the re-entrant, go faster than those breasting the slope. The result is a wedge. Moreover, the wedge is led by breastplated officers wielding sword and halberd, and the bulk of their followers are musketeers.

The first clash was encouraging for the Royalists. Walker wrote, 'The Foot on either side hardly saw each other until they were within Carabine Shot, and so made only one Volley; ours falling in with Sword and butt end of the Musquet did notable Execution; so much as I saw their colours fall, and the Foot in great Disorder.' He also reported that both guns and muskets of the Parliamentarians had fired high, so the attack was not checked by firearms. Sprigge said, 'The Enemy this while marched up in good order, a swift march, with a great deal of gallantry and resolution...' The involuntary wedge of attackers struck Waller's little regiment and Pickering's larger formation, leaving Skippon's men isolated on higher ground to the west and possibly part of Montagu's similarly placed on the east. The hilltop has yielded up the evidence of a belt of musket shot some 675 yards wide, which leaves Skippon's left and most of Fairfax's foot untargeted, for it is clear that there was small opportunity for further gunfire in this place; only hand-to-hand fighting was possible. Sprigge's account tells of the crisis his side endured:

The right hand of the Foot, being the General's [Fairfax's] Regiment, stood, not being much pressed upon: Almost all the rest of the main Battail being overpressed, gave ground and went off in some disorder, falling behind the Reserves; but the Colonels and Officers, doing the duty of very gallant Men, in endeavouring to keep their men from disorder...

OKEY'S DRAGOONS (pages 68–69)

Cromwell had observed that the northern end of the hedge enclosing Sulby parish flanked Prince Maurice's infantry at the point at which it turned westwards. The hedge (1) was both old and substantial, for the fields had probably been enclosed as early as 1428, and in 1547 there were 2,000 sheep being grazed here. It was thus stock-proof and in June would give good cover from sight, though not, of course, from musket fire. The hedge still runs up to the top of Dust Hill ridge from the valley where the stream marking the Naseby–Sibbertoft boundary sluggishly flows, at that time through marshy ground. Okey lost no time in taking his men through the access from the green lane at the south-western corner and northwards to get in range of his enemies. What he may not have known was that the Royalist horse was accompanied by musketeers who could not but have seen the dragoons

as they came down the far slope and picked their way across the boggy bottom land before resuming their gallop. As Okey's men dismounted, every tenth man being given charge of the mounts of nine of his comrades (2), the reins of one over the head of the next, and prepared to attack, the Royalist muskets blazed a volley through the hedge, firing blind. The dragoons (3) fell back some distance down the slope and opened fire on the Royalist horse (4), which stood some time, as musket-ball finds show, before being forced forwards in some disorder, off the hill, and into the valley where they were able to re-form and launch their change on Ireton's horse. Okey had precipitated the start of the fight. Beyond the hedge the corners of the colonel of the Earl of Northampton's Regiment of Horse can be seen on the right. The corner on the left is that of the Queen's Regiment of Horse, which was taken at Naseby.

The road from Dust Hill to Naseby, from Broadmoor. The hedge-line with the Cromwell Monument now forms the horizon on the right, and to the left is the frontage available to Cromwell. Lodge Hill is the field on the skyline on the extreme left. The nearer one gets to that ridge, the less one can see what is on top of it.

The front line did not hold, and the Parliamentarian centre fell back behind the second line. On the right was Colonel Thomas Rainsborough's (888 men, State Paper figures) with Colonel Robert Hammond's (788) to his left and then Lieutenant-Colonel Thomas Pride's (1,151) of which half was in the second line and the other half in the rear, probably along the little ridge that connects the Closter Hill ridge, off which they were being forced, with the Mill Hill ridge. On the extreme left Skippon's men fought on, mixed with some of Ireton's cavalry, and with their commanding officer courageously remaining on the field in spite of a musket-ball wound in his side, probably 'friendly fire'. George Bishop, 'a Gentleman in the Army' wrote, 'In the first charge he received his wound, shot through the right side under the ribbes, through Armour, and Coat, but not mortall, yet notwithstanding hee kept his Horse, and discharged his place, and would by no means bee drawn off til the Field was wonne; for the space of two hours and a half.'

THE TURN OF THE TIDE

The outnumbered Royalists had failed to make a breakthrough and were now battling within a salient driven into their enemy's front. As fatigue ate into their vigour they endured enfilading assaults from their flanks and the impact of the fresh Parliamentary reserves on their front. Meanwhile the cavalry action on the east had developed in Cromwell's favour. Langdale's horse, the Northern Horse in the front line, moved to the attack and Cromwell's moved forwards to meet them. That the heat and burden of the day fell upon Whalley's and Pye's men is clear from the fact that the former suffered 50 casualties and the latter 44, whereas Cromwell's to their right sustained only 24 and the rest between them a mere 11. The frontage between Fairfax's foot and the boggy valley beyond Lodge Hill included the rabbit warren on the latter, so that the attackers could not charge onto that ground, nor could Cromwell's men charge off it. The heavy fighting took place in the

THE ROYALIST RETREAT, SECOND PHASE

The battle across Broadmoor on 14 June 1645, as seen from the west. The Royalist assault has broken Parliament's left wing of horse and penetrated the front line of foot, but the assault on the right wing of horse has been thrown back. Much of the fighting becomes confused and some formations mingle. Lacking reinforcements, the Royalists are compelled to retreat.

Note: Gridlines are shown at intervals of 1,000m/1,094yds

LODGE HILL

DUST HILL

ROYALIST FORCES

The Right Wing of Horse
A Prince Rupert's and Prince Maurice's Lifeguards.
B Prince Rupert's Regiment
C The Queen's and Prince Maurice's Regiments
D The Earl of Northampton's Regiment
E Sir William Vaughan's Regiment

The Foot
Sir Bernard Astley's Tertia of Foot
F The Duke of York's Regiment
G Sir Edward Hopton's Regiment
H Sir Richard Page's Regiment
Bard's Tertia
I Sir Henry Bard's Regiment and the Queen's Lifeguard
J Sir John Owen's and Col Radcliffe Gerard's Regiments

Sir George Lisle's Tertia
K Sir George Lisle's and Col St George's Regiments
L The Shrewsbury Foot (Broughton's, Tillier's, Hunks's, Warren's and Gibson's Regiments)

Three Divisions of Horse
M, N Bagot's and Leveson's
O Col Thomas Howard's

The Left Wing of Horse
P, Q, R The Northern Horse, three divisions under Sir Marmaduke Langdale
S Sir Horatio Carey's Regiment
T Northern Horse, one division under Sir William Balckiston

The Reserve
U, V The Newark Horse
W The Lifeguard of Foot
X The King's Lifeguard of Horse
Y Prince Rupert's Bluecoat Regiment of Foot

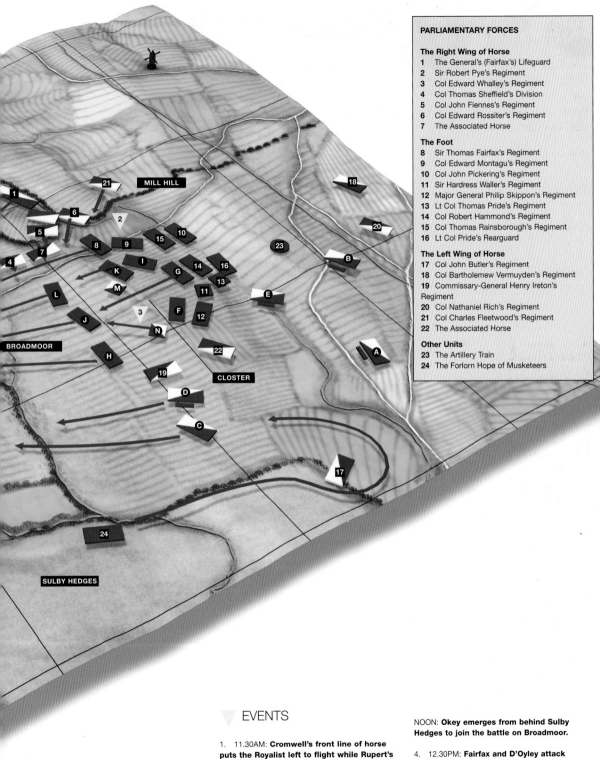

PARLIAMENTARY FORCES

The Right Wing of Horse
1 The General's (Fairfax's) Lifeguard
2 Sir Robert Pye's Regiment
3 Col Edward Whalley's Regiment
4 Col Thomas Sheffield's Division
5 Col John Fiennes's Regiment
6 Col Edward Rossiter's Regiment
7 The Associated Horse

The Foot
8 Sir Thomas Fairfax's Regiment
9 Col Edward Montagu's Regiment
10 Col John Pickering's Regiment
11 Sir Hardress Waller's Regiment
12 Major General Philip Skippon's Regiment
13 Lt Col Thomas Pride's Regiment
14 Col Robert Hammond's Regiment
15 Col Thomas Rainsborough's Regiment
16 Lt Col Pride's Rearguard

The Left Wing of Horse
17 Col John Butler's Regiment
18 Col Bartholemew Vermuyden's Regiment
19 Commissary-General Henry Ireton's Regiment
20 Col Nathaniel Rich's Regiment
21 Col Charles Fleetwood's Regiment
22 The Associated Horse

Other Units
23 The Artillery Train
24 The Forlorn Hope of Musketeers

▼ EVENTS

1. 11.30AM: **Cromwell's front line of horse puts the Royalist left to flight while Rupert's Bluecoats move forwards to Dust Hill.**

2. 11.30AM: **Cromwell's second line of horse wheels left against the Royalist infantry flank.**

3. NOON: **The Royalist foot falls back. Many of them are surrounded and taken prisoner on Broadmoor. Others begin a fighting withdrawal from the field.**

NOON: **Okey emerges from behind Sulby Hedges to join the battle on Broadmoor.**

4. 12.30PM: **Fairfax and D'Oyley attack Rupert's Bluecoats at front and rear and overcome them.**

5. 1.00PM: **The Royalists retreat, fighting a rearguard action, regiments giving covering fire and retreating, turn and turn about. Fairfax restrains the pursuit and follows with horse and foot together.**

narrow passage between the foot and the warren, and the tired and homesick men of the Northern Horse gave good account of themselves, as the casualties inflicted bear witness.

Walker wrote, 'Yet I must needs say ours did as well as the Place and their Number would admit; but being flanked and pressed back, they at last gave their ground and fled...' The speed with which Cromwell's reserves could move forwards was also limited by the need to pass through the narrow gap vacated by Whalley's two divisions and the single front line division of Pye's regiment and moreover the degree of control required from Cromwell in order to retain reserves to charge the foot was that much less. Slingsby, who was probably involved himself, wrote:

> But our Northern horse who stood upon yt wing, & ye Newark horse ... being out front'd & overpoure'd by their assailants, after they were close joyn'd, they stood a pretty while, & neither seem'd to yield, till more came up on their flanks & put ym to rout, & wheeling to our right took ym in disorder, & so presently made our whole horse to run...

Rupert's journal relates 'The P[rince] came back to the reserve and found the King's regiment and the P[rince]'s regiment of foot etc.' and this passage carries a marginal note that says 'The Yorkshire horse was gone without fighting,' which is clearly untrue. However, it continues, 'The King had sent away by some bodyes persuasion about him all his horse to charge the wing of the horse of the enemy, whereas if they had stayed till the P[rince] came back, and marched horse and foot together, they had probably beaten them.' It would therefore seem that the reserves of horse in the Royalist centre had also been thrown in, which is perhaps why Symonds, in the King's Lifeguard of Horse, said, 'wee marched up to them through a bottome full off furse [gorse] bushes; they shott two peices of cannon, wee one: one of their was at the King's body of horse, where he was before.'

Sprigge's story was:

> ...Col. Whaley's Division routed those two Divisions of Langdales, driving them back to Prince Ruperts Regiment, being the Reserve of the enemies Foot, whither indeed they fled for shelter, and rallied... In the mean time, the rest of the Divisions of the Right wing, being straightned by Furzes on the right hand, advanced with great difficulty, as also by reason of the unevennesse of the ground, and a Cony-warren [rabbit warren] over which they were to march, which put them somewhat out of their order...

The constraint of the warren and the gorse or furze clearly slowed the advance of the right of Cromwell's front, and thus made the control of the reserves easier; terrain rather than discipline held the horse in check so that part of the second line could be ordered to wheel left on the Royalist foot's flank and the rest used in an organized assault on the remnants of Langdale's horse. 'Notwithstanding which difficulty, they came up to the engaging the residue of the Enemies horse on the left wing, whom they routed...' There is evidence on the forward slope towards the eastern end of Dust Hill of a sustained fight, with some of the heaviest shotfall yet found and it seems likely that this marks the place that Rupert's Bluecoat Regiment of Foot gave shelter to the remnants of the cavalry.

Text at top of sketch (handwritten): *...crossing the Sibbertoft road, and getting up close to Clostercell (which takes up Lodge Hill to the West) you look down over Broadmoor. Not a quarter of a mile from this spot is the Grave mealing... behind: to the South West higher up the Hill... was not this the thickest point of the Fight?*

Labels on sketch: *Dust Hill Farm*, *Sibbertoft*, *Broad Moor.*, *Clostercell*, *the crook in this hedge where dead are laid by*, *Sibbertoft Road.*

THE FIGHTING RETREAT

On Closter Hill the Parliamentarian reserves were now pushing their attackers back, and with the collapse of the Northern Horse, Walker relates, 'Four of the Rebels Bodies [of horse] close and in good Order followed them, the rest charged our foot.' The Royalist foot fell back across Broadmoor, going the way they had come, with the hopeful solidity of the Bluecoats securing the road northwards. The survivors of Ireton's wing, possibly commanded by Fleetwood, had rallied and having circumnavigated their infantry by the south, formed up as a further reinforcement to Cromwell's force. Fairfax had been on the move throughout the fight and Bishop claims that he was involved in Cromwell's successful action 'In which the Generall charged valiantly, and lost his Head-piece, who seeing the left scattered, he with Lieutenant-Generall Cromwell faced about to that Wing, with some Divisions of Horse, charged bareheaded within push of Pike, routed the Enemy...'

Bulstrode Whitelocke also reported that Fairfax had had his helmet knocked off. The general happened upon the commander of his troop of Lifeguard, Colonel Charles D'Oyley, and was rebuked for his lack of protection and offered D'Oyley's helmet. This he declined, but asked if D'Oyley had attacked the body of Royalist foot, probably the Bluecoats, still standing unbroken. 'Twice,' was the answer. 'With that, Fairfax bid him to charge them once again in the front, and that he would take a commanded party, and charge them in the rear...' The Bluecoats were already enduring the assault of Fairfax's infantry and the position on Dust Hill is marked with shot along the parish boundary and more shot along the top of the slope, as of a regiment attacked fore and aft. Sprigge wrote:

> *...the remaining business was with part to keep the enemies horse coming to the rescue of their foot, which were now all at mercy, except one Tertia, which with the other part of the horse we endeavoured to break but could not ... until such time as the Generall called up his own Regiment of foot...*

The *Kingdoms Weekly Intelligencer* of 10–17 June reported, 'The Blue regiment of the Kings stood to it very stoutly, and stir'd not, like a wall of brasse, though encompassed by our Forces, so that our men were forced to knock them down with the But end of their Musquets...' The

THE LAST STAND

During the afternoon of 14 June 1645 the Royalists were driven back to a final, organized stand on Wadborough Hill, overlooking the Welland Valley, while fleeing followers from the baggage train were caught, robbed and brutalized in the enclosed field of Nobold Closes. Regimental identities are not known and much of the fighting was broken at this stage, so few fixed troop positions are shown and the timing is entirely conjectural. The terrain is shown looking south, towards Naseby.

Note: Gridlines are shown at intervals of 1,000m/1,094yds.

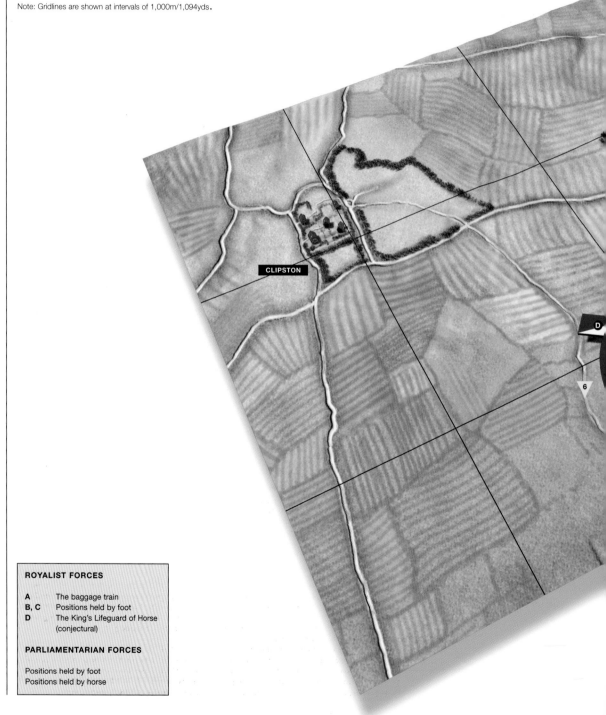

CLIPSTON

D

6

ROYALIST FORCES

A   The baggage train
B, C   Positions held by foot
D   The King's Lifeguard of Horse
       (conjectural)

PARLIAMENTARIAN FORCES

Positions held by foot
Positions held by horse

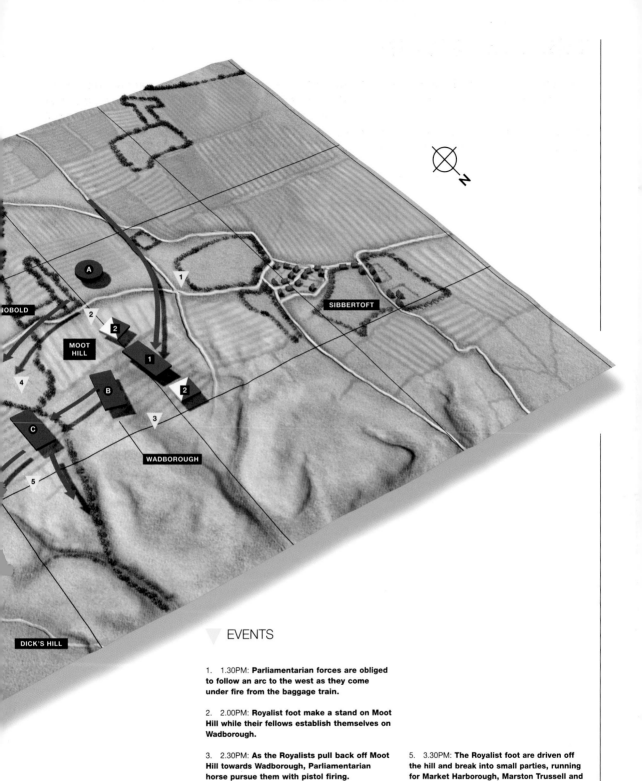

OBOLD

SIBBERTOFT

MOOT
HILL

A

B

C

WADBOROUGH

DICK'S HILL

1

2

2

2

1

2

3

4

5

▼ EVENTS

1.   1.30PM: **Parliamentarian forces are obliged to follow an arc to the west as they come under fire from the baggage train.**

2.   2.00PM: **Royalist foot make a stand on Moot Hill while their fellows establish themselves on Wadborough.**

3.   2.30PM: **As the Royalists pull back off Moot Hill towards Wadborough, Parliamentarian horse pursue them with pistol firing.**

4.   3.00PM: **Heavy fighting ensues across the narrow valley between Moot Hill and Wadborough. Fleeing Royalist followers encounter traffic still attempting to turn back on the Clipston road and spill into the close north of the road in an attempt to run away through the gate in the parish boundary.**

5.   3.30PM: **The Royalist foot are driven off the hill and break into small parties, running for Market Harborough, Marston Trussell and the roads northwards, turning and firing from time to time as they go.**

6.   3.30PM: **Maybe here the King is tempted to lead his Lifeguard in a final charge, but is restrained and his horse's head turned for flight towards Market Harborough and the river crossing at Bloodyman's Ford.**

final charge of horse brought Fairfax and D'Oyley together in the midst of them and the general himself slew the ensign. One of D'Oyley's troopers took the colours and crowed his prowess, but when his officer took him to task Fairfax said 'I have honour enough, let him take that to himself.' The *Intelligencer* continued, 'It is conceived that a great part of them were Irish, and chose rather to die in the field than be hanged.' If that was the motivation for fighting to the death it would not apply to the Bluecoats, but might indicate the presence of the Shrewsbury Foot, made up of regiments originally raised in Dublin, though few Irish would be with them by this time.

At this point traditional accounts speak of the Royalist flight to Leicester without further ado. The archaeological evidence proves a different tale, but one hard to relate to the eyewitness accounts we have. The need to guess at intervals of time makes the reconstruction of events more tenuous, although it is necessary to try. All the way north, as far as the Sibbertoft to Clipston road, bands of shot lie across the route, suggesting a recurrent firefight, men turning to loose a volley on their pursuers and covering the retreat of their comrades before themselves falling back under the covering fire of others. There were officers here who had commanded a similar retreat at Cheriton and these were seasoned men that they commanded. At the junction with the Kelmarsh road the shot begins to make a huge arc, turning clockwise to the east as it crosses the Clipston road, fire emanating, it would seem, from the Royalist baggage train to their right. Some evidence has been found of a fight west of Sibbertoft as well, perhaps from another section of the train which had come up from Husbands Bosworth. The flag marking the route from East Farndon had flown, or perhaps was still flying, on Moot Hill, to which this scatter of shot leads, and here another phase of resistance flared up. How long it lasted one cannot say, but the eastern slope has nothing but pistol shot: a cavalry attack on fleeing foot. Clarendon's *History* remarks, 'About three miles northward off the scene of action, near the Moot-hill just above Farndon, a small party off the

Looking north-east to Moot Hill from the Sibbertoft to Clipston road over the line of flight and pursuit. The retreating Royalists ran down the hill and up across the location of the circular copse on the left to make a stand on the hilltop, centre. The lone tree on the horizon on the right can be seen for miles, and is close to the probable location of the standard raised to mark the line of march. (John Kliene)

Kinge's armie made a halt, drew up into a body, and seemed resolute on renewing the engagement, but quickly retired on the approach of the enemie...' The control exercised by Parliamentarian officers was strict and effective, according to Sprigge, 'It was ordered our horse should not come up to charge the enemy until the foot were come up ... [our horse] were again put in two wings, within Carbine shot of the enemy, leaving a wide space for the battail of foot to fall in...' Both these accounts suggest that the very threat of a fresh assault by the New Model Army was sufficient to send the Royalists off in flight, but the substantial finds of shot on the ground prove otherwise.

THE FINAL PHASE

Between Moot Hill and Wadborough, the next height to the east, the valley was thick with shot laid down as two forces stood opposed on opposite sides. To the south were the thick hedges of another enclosure, 'Englands', the inland stockholding field of the deserted village of Nobold, and beyond it the road between Clipston and Sibbertoft, now jammed with fugitive Royalist camp followers. The pursuing horse could not get through the hedges and the Royalist flank on Wadborough was therefore protected, but not just by the hedges; the field was filled with running women and servants, referred to by 'a Gentleman in Northampton' as 'the middle sort of Ammunition Whoores, whoe were full of money and rich apparel, there being 1500 of that tribe...' unable to escape by the road and seeking to get away through the gate on the Clipston side. Many failed. John Rushworth wrote the next day, 'the Irish women Prince Rupert brought upon the field ... our souldiers would grant no quarter too, about 100 slain of them, and most of the rest of the whores that attended that wicked Army are marked in the face or nose, with a slash or cut.'

To the north of Wadborough the shot traces grow more slender as fewer survived to resist, but show the routes men followed towards East Farndon, Market Harborough and Marston Trussell, turning and fighting and running to turn and fight again.

At some point, perhaps here, maybe earlier in the day, the king was tempted to intervene personally. Walker recounted immediately after telling of Cromwell's rout of Langdale:

> At this instant the King's Horse-guards and the King at the Head of them were ready to charge those who followed ours, when a person of Quality, 'tis said the Earl of Carnwath, took the King's Horse by the Bridle, turned him about, swearing at him and saying, Will you go upon your Death? And at the same time the Word being given, March to the right Hand ... we turned about and ran on the Spur almost quarter of a Mile, and then the Word being given to make a Stand, we did so; though the Body could never be rallyed. Those that came back made a Charge, wherein some of them fell.

There are few places from which an order to move to the right would result in a movement compatible with the shape of the action as revealed by the archaeology, but the movement from Moot Hill to

ENGLANDS AND WADBOROUGH (pages 80–81)

The fighting retreat retraced the Royalist approach route, over Moot Hill, where a stand was made while men occupied Wadborough (1) to give covering fire to their comrades in the next phase of the withdrawal. The Royalist baggage train on the other side of the lane from Clipston to Sibbertoft was cut off and a flight back down the lane proved impossible as arriving traffic blocked the sunken road. Desperate camp followers, respectable ladies and 'the middle sort of Ammunition Whoores' alike rushed across the enclosed field, 'Englands', north of the lane, in an attempt to flee through the Clipston gate (2) towards East Farndon. Rushworth wrote '... the Irish women ... our souldiers would grant no quarter too, about 100 slain of them, and most of the rest of the whores ... are marked in the face or nose, with a slash or cut.' Those with a purse were, if lucky, merely robbed. Fairfax had kept his horse and foot together in the pursuit, but here the temptation of loot has led a trooper (3), a dragoon (4) and a musketeer (5) of Fairfax's regiment to assault the fugitives. From the hill above what fire the Royalist remnants could muster was directed at the assault coming from the valley below Moot Hill. the colours of Sir George Lisle's Regiment and the King's Lifeguard of Foot can be seen. It was the last substantial resistance; from Wadborough they broke into smaller parties and, while more fighting took place all the way to Leicester, the Parliamentarian task was now to mop up a defeated enemy.

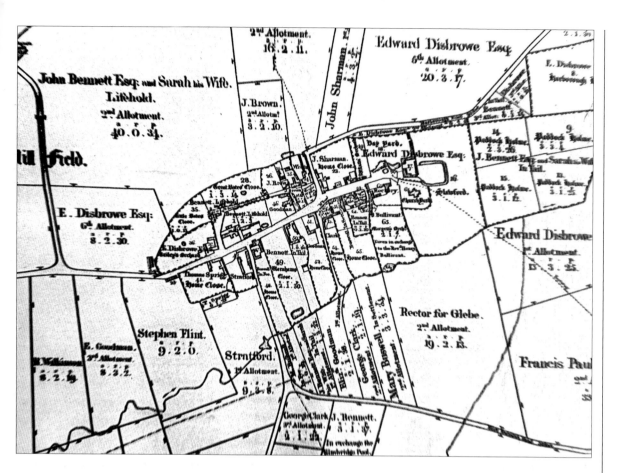

Marston Trussell in 1815. The road from the battlefield entered the High Street from the bottom of the map and that for Market Harborough top right, but this required a left turn into a narrow road while a broad route forwards beckoned. It led, however, to a dead end at the church. (Northampton Record Office, 28676B)

Wadborough or from Wadborough to Dick's Hill and thence to flight might fit. Another record which perhaps relates comes from Okey: 'Cromwell his Regiment drave the Enemy before them; which I perceiving (after one houre's battail) caused all my men to mount and to charge into their Foot, which accordingly they did; and took all their Colours, and 500 Prisoners, besides what wee killed, and all their Armes.' But Okey had to emerge from behind Sulby Hedges, riding south to get out and turning north to fall on the fleeing foot, probably on Dust Hill or the road north of that. Then, he says, 'After this the King his Horse drew up into a body againe: and then I drew up my Dragoons, and charged the King's Regiment of Horse, and they faced about and run away and never made any stay till they came to Leicester...' If he is truthful or, more kindly, accurate, in this it might have been Okey's Dragoons that, having started the fight, finished it on Wadborough.

Slingsby made good his escape. 'The way I took was upon my right hand, leaving Harborrow on my left ... wn all ours besides took Harborrow on ye right & were come to Leister long before we got thither.' Mounted fugitives obviously had a better chance of escape, but it was reported in *The Moderate Intelligencer* of 12–19 June that the king was nearly taken prisoner as he rode away. As is natural, his party was retracing its steps to Market Harborough, making for the ford over the River Welland through which they had marched so optimistically that morning. From the account it appears that the Parliamentarian horse had cut them off:

Other horsemen attempted to flee by way of Marston Trussell, where some had been billeted the night before and where the church reared prominently above the fields. Here, local tales asserted, Royalists had been caught and cut down after the battle, and therefore, in 1842, Edward Fitzgerald went to investigate. He wrote to Thomas Carlyle on 30 September to report his findings. 'I drove my gig into Marston, straight along the road from Sibbertoft, to the Church: where, at the very church yard gate, the road stopped: went no farther.' It was, he explained, a 'Pudding-bay-end' or 'cul-de-sac'. The parson told Fitzgerald that the field beyond was called Slawford, meaning Slaughterford, and that his father had, when digging to make a family vault, come upon a mass burial. Today the road continues past the church and the dog-leg of the old road can be traced in the bridle path that leads north off the high street, and the village name 'Pudding-bag Marston' is just a memory.

Those who came to Leicester did not stay long. Slingsby wrote, 'Ye King made no stay at Leister but march'd presently to Ashby Delazuch; ... ye next day, being Sunday, we [Slingsby with Lords Bellasyse and Beamond] came to ye King at Ashby, a Garison well stor'd wth good victuals & a good Cellar.'

From the Royal Observer Corps post next to Dick's Hill, the Clipston to Marston Trussell road, a view across the scene of the closing phase of the battle. The lone tree on Moot Hill is in the centre, on the skyline, and to its right the retreat came down the slope to where the hedge runs out of sight on the parish boundary onto Wadborough, the nearer hill, on which the final, organized resistance was offered. To the left the bare earth of 'Englands' lies below Lowe Farm on the Sibbertoft to Clipston road, and here it is supposed that the atrocities were committed on Royalist followers. (John Kliene)

The 'Gentleman in Northampton' toured the field after the battle and wrote on 15 June:

The Field was about a mile broad where the Battell was fought, and from the outmost Flanke of the right, to the left wing, tooke up the whole ground; The bodies lay slaine about four miles in length, the most thicke on the hill the Kings men stood on; I cannot think there was few lesse than four hundred men slaine, and truly I think not many more, and neere 300 Horses; Wee tooke at least four thousand Prisoners on the ground between Navesby and Harborough, neere three hundred carriages, whereof twelve of them were Ordnance ... there was many of the Wagons laden with rich plunder, and others with Arms and Ammunition...

AFTERMATH

The losses sustained by Charles I's army at Naseby were immense. On the field of battle, Sprigge said:

> *The number of the slain we had not a certain account of by reason of the prosecution of our victory ... prisoners taken in the field were about five thousand ... the whole booty of the Field fell to the Souldier, which was very rich and considerable, there being amongst it, besides the riches of the Court, and Officers, the rich plunder of Leicester. Their Train of Artillery was taken, all their Ordnance ... eight thousand Arms and more, forty Barrels of powder, two hundred horse ... the Kings Cabinet ... many Coaches...*

Rushworth stated, 'I viewed the dead bodies, from the Battel to Harborough truly I estimate them not to be above 700, together with those slain in the running away, but in pursuit between Harborough and Leicester, and by townes, conceived about 300 more slain, abundance wounded...'

The treatment of the wounded had, by this time, become comparatively sophisticated under the provisions made by Parliament. Many of the men injured at Naseby were moved to Northampton in the days after the battle and 40 Parliamentary troops were treated at St John's Hospital in Bridge Street. Skippon was carried to Mr Stanley's house in Brixworth where Dr Clark from Wellingborough treated him. The general became fevered, presumably because of the infection of his wound, but by 25 June was on the mend. The great number of patients required the services of at least nine surgeons to assist the Surgeon-General Daniel Winter and money was granted for the continuing care of about 450 Parliamentary men in Northampton, of whom 41 died. Some of the severely wounded were transported to London by one Thomas Campion who had four nurses to attend to them. Most of the Royalist wounded were taken to Market Harborough, Rockingham or Northampton where All Saints and other churches were used to house 500 of them. Four carts full of Royalist wounded went to London with other prisoners where they arrived on 21 June and were taken to the Military Ground behind St James's Palace for treatment.

The loss of men and supplies of arms and ammunition was a severe blow to the Royalists, but added to that was the loss of the king's Cabinet, his personal correspondence not only with his council and generals, but also with the queen, who was soliciting reinforcements on the Continent. This was published 'by speciall Order of the Parliament' as soon as possible, perhaps in July, under the title of *The Kings Cabinet Opened*, which made the most of every opportunity to show the author of these letters as a Catholic sympathizer at the best and as a traitor to the independence of the English at the worst. A clergyman called Edward

The capture of Charles's correspondence after the battle provided Parliament with a propaganda coup that was exploited immediately. (Naseby Battlefield Project)

Supporters of the king responded to *The King's Cabinet Opened* with *A Vindication of King Charles*.

Symmons immediately set about refuting the charges, writing *A Vindication of King Charles* in Cornwall, but before he could finish it 'the Enemy, like a flood, brake in thither: Whereupon to preserve and finish it, I went to France...' The work eventually appeared in 1648 and is as full of bias and special pleading as the work it proposed to refute.

HINDSIGHT

In the weeks immediately after the battle the attempts to explain or to blame began. Both sides claimed the approval of the Almighty in their enterprises, and failure was therefore something luck or circumstance alone was insufficient to justify. Rupert was well aware of the inevitable attempts to put the onus of defeat on him. He wrote to Will Legge on 18 June from Bewdley, to tell him he had sent reinforcements to him in the shape of Northampton's and Thomas Howard's regiments and went on to ask:

> *Pray lett me knowe what is said among you concerning our last defeat; doubtlesse the faulte of it will be put upon Rup: – I sent you word of the truthe in my last from Wolverhampton... Since this businesse, I find Dickby hath omitted nothinge wch might prejudice Rup; and this day has drawne a letter for the King to Pr: Charls, in which, he crosses, all things, which befell here, in Rup:s behalf. I have shew'd this to King; – and in ernest, if hereupon he should goe on, and send it, I shall be forced to quit my Genlship...*

It would be instructive to have the letter from Wolverhampton.

On 30 June Digby wrote to Legge from Hereford in an attempt to recruit him to the ranks of Rupert's critics. It was a flattering missive, suggesting that had Legge himself been present at Naseby he would have been able at least to question certain decisions that Digby implies cost them the victory. Digby goes on to say, with what sincerity the reader may judge:

> *As to the particular aspersion upon him [Prince Rupert], which you mention, of fightinge against advise, Hee is very much wronged in it; wheither you meane in the generall or in the particular of that day; for in the generall when contrarye to the advise of soe many, it was once resolved that wee should march the way wee did, it was then the unanimous opinion of all, that if Fairfax should follow us neare, wee ought to turne upon him, and fight with him, before he could joine with the Scotts. And the particular time, place and circumstances of our fightinge that day, – His Highns cannot be sayd to have gone against my Lord Astley's or any mans advise, for I am confidend noe mans was askt upon the occasion I am sure noe councell called. I shall onlye say this freely to you, that I thinke, a principall occasion of our misfortune was, the want of you wth us; for had you beene there, I am persuaded that when once wee were come upp soe neere them, as that they could not goe from us, you would at least have askt some questions, wheither havinge store of provisions with us, wee should not rather have tried to bring them to our posts, than to have assaulted them instantlye in theirs. That if it were resolved wee must assaile them, you would have askt*

the question wheither it had not been fitt rather to have advanced to, or gained some place, where our cannon might have beene of use, rather than to have drawne upp a hill against them, soe as never to make use of one peece; and lastlye, that before we joined Battailes, wheither it would not have beene convenient to have viewed the Enemyes strength, & posture, rather then to have left it to this hower in dispute; wheither the Enemye had not 3000 men behinde in reserve, more than those wee fought with (which Sr Wm Vaughan whoe charged quite through those bodyes wch were in our Eye positively affirmed) I make no doubt you would alsoe have asked some materiall questions concerning a reserve, & the Placinge of the Kings person where it should not have been suddainlye involved in the first confusion. But reallye my Deare Will: I doe not write this with reflexion, for indeed wee were all carried on at that time, with such a speritt and confidence of victory, as hee that should have say'd consider, would have been our foe; and soe did our fate leade us, as scarce the wisest of us did thinke of a queere [query], or objection then which after the ill successe, every Child could light on.

The end of the letter was not lacking a further sting:

Give your Prince good advise, as to Caution, and value of Councell, and God will yet make him an Instrument of much happynesse to the Kinge, and Kingdome, and that being, I will adore him, as much as you love him, though he should hate
    Your faithfullest friend & servant.
    George Digbye.

The answer to the above, which is in the transcription of the earl of Dartmouth's collection of originals made by Lord Bagot in 1816 and

Etching by Jan Luyken (1649–1712) with a later colouring depicting the execution of Charles I on 30 January 1649. (Copyright Akg-images)

1817, appears in Eliot Warburton's work of 1849. Legge clearly does not fall for Digby's line and, with all the respect he can summon, says:

...truly, my Lord, your last letter to me gives me some cause to think your Lordship not altogether free from what he often accused you of as the reason of his jealousies; which was, that you did both say and do things to his prejudice contrary to your professions, not in an open and direct line, but obscurely and obliquely; and this way, under your Lordship's pardon, I find your letter, in my understanding, very full of.

He goes on to point out that waiting for the enemy would have attracted even greater condemnation, that the attempts of both sides to make the best of the ground were widely reported and that as a result of these attempts neither side, in the end, was able to make significant use of cannon.

And for viewing the enemy, to be satisfied in their number and posture, I will not say but, could it be done, it would have been very fit before both armies were face to face. I am sure it might have been too late then to have stood upon the ceremony.

The existence of the reserve is asserted and the matter of the king's position is, he points out, a question for his immediate Council. Legge closes with the observation that 'you are not free from great blame towards Prince Rupert...'

As to the campaign as a whole, Edward Wogan wrote of his adversaries' strategy:

If the King had but kept from engaging his army but one month (which he might easily have done) we were certainly undone. The army in the West would be lost... All the North would have done their endeavour for him; and so would the Associated Counties: and I believe the Scots would have declared for him, or at least stood neuters...

Of the unexpected on the battlefield itself, only the bad ground on Cromwell's front, namely the rabbit warren, bog and gorse, receives consistent mention as a factor influencing the outcome. The critical decision to send Okey up behind Sulby Hedges and thus precipitate the Royalist cavalry charge is not given its true importance in determining the commencement and subsequent course of battle. The dip in the ridge on the Parliamentarian foot's frontage is not mentioned by any contemporary writer and only evinces itself to someone walking the ground at leisure, an opportunity denied at the time, but it led inexorably to the crisis that Skippon and his regimental commanders had to overcome. Two interesting considerations emerge from Digby's effort to discredit Rupert. First, he confirms that Vaughan found the Parliamentarian flank unassailable and the reserves substantial, which suggests that the horse was in fact meant to wheel and attack that rear flank having broken Ireton's front. Second, he makes no mention of Rupert having absented himself for an undue period, while, as other accounts assert, he was sacking the baggage train or calling on the artillery train to surrender. Thus Digby himself supports, by implication, the vindication of Rupert's plans and actions on the Royalist right wing.

THE FORTUNES OF THE KING

Fairfax retook Leicester on 18 June. Charles I made for the Welsh Marches and, Goring having been defeated by Fairfax at Langport on 10 July, Rupert prepared to defend Bristol. The king then set off from Cardiff and, leaving Lord Leven's Scots besieging Hereford, made for Litchfield and Doncaster where, on 19 August, Symonds records that his strength was 2,200 horse and 400 foot. But he was now in peril from pursuing Scots and approaching Parliamentarians from the North and so turned back to Oxford and in September was back at Raglan Castle.

On 4 September Fairfax summoned Rupert to surrender Bristol. On 10 September Fairfax assaulted the place. It soon became apparent that it could not be held and that if resistance continued the slaughter would be extreme. Rupert therefore surrendered on terms that allowed his army to leave with their weapons and colours and be granted the dignity of an escort to Oxford. The king was furious and was persuaded to strip his nephew of his rank and appointments. In a dramatic foray, Rupert forced his way into the king's presence in Newark in mid-October, demanding a court martial, which, granted, found him not guilty. It was not until December that a reconciliation was achieved, but by then the Royalist cause was, in military terms, lost. On 21 March 1646 the last Royalist field army, under Lord Astley, was defeated at Stow-on-the-Wold. On 27 April the king left Oxford in disguise on his way to Newark, where he hoped to persuade the Scots to espouse his cause. They did not. On 5 May Charles rode into their headquarters at Southwell and gave himself up. Oxford, the Royalist capital, was surrendered on 20 June.

A portrait of Oliver Cromwell from *The Emblem of England's Distraction* (1658) in which the hero is shown trampling Error and Faction underfoot while in the foreground are figures symbolic of swords having been beaten into ploughshares and spears into pruning hooks. Numerous other symbolic images complete the page.

THE BATTLEFIELD TODAY

At the time of writing two monuments stand outside Naseby. The Obelisk on the road to Clipston was erected on the old windmill mound and the Cromwell Monument on the road to Sibbertoft stands north of the Parliamentary front line overlooking Broadmoor. In the late 1990s a group of local residents sought the support of the Battlefields Trust in their desire to improve the presentation and interpretation of the field of battle at Naseby, and in 2005 the initiative gained the support of Northamptonshire County Council. Works to realize the plans began in 2006. Visiting the area requires caution lest one interfere with farmers and others going about their business and care must be taken not to block gates or narrow roads.

Access to the battle area can be had from junctions 1 or 2 of the A14. If travelling to the region north along the M1, note that there is no exit to the A14 at junction 19; it is necessary to continue to junction 20 and return south to 19 or to head east on the A4304 to Market Harborough and turn south for East Farndon at Welland Park. The London (St Pancras) to Leicester railway line passes through Market Harborough and the Jurassic Way long-distance path goes through Sulby and Sibbertoft.

The Obelisk, when a windmill stood there, was the rendezvous for the Parliamentarian army on 14 June 1645 and from it the East Farndon ridge is not visible. From a position north of the A14 before the road drops down towards Clipston, the tree-edged East Farndon to Little Oxendon road can be seen on the distant ridge, marking the rear of the Royalists' initial deployment, and to the west Lowe Farm is prominent near Sibbertoft Wood, showing the location of Moot Hill and Wadborough, the route of the Royalists' advance and retreat. Farther west the Dust Hill ridge north of Broadmoor is indicated by the buildings of Prince Rupert's Farm and Dust Hill Farm. This viewpoint is close to the position from which Fairfax and Cromwell evaluated the situation before making the decision to move west to do battle.

The Royalist position was at first just south of East Farndon and from it they looked south in vain. Today a radio mast indicates the route of the A14 and west of it the Naseby to Clipston road coming over the ridge can be picked out: Fairfax's position is described above. Farther west the spire of Naseby church shows over trees on the skyline (the church had only a tower in 1645). From this place Moot Hill and Lowe Farm are on a skyline, which is why a flag was required to guide the army's movement.

From the Cromwell Monument on the Naseby to Sibbertoft road, looking northwards, the Royalist position before the fight can be seen. On the left is Prince Rupert's Farm, to the west of which was the right wing of the horse. On the right the brick of Dust Hill Farm and the trees of Longhold Spinney to the east show where the left wing of horse was positioned, and the foot were in between. On the far left, the west, the

line of Sulby Hedges can, with some difficulty, be picked out. The straight line of the 19th-century enclosure road runs north on the right, curving only where it crosses the parish boundary to Sibbertoft. To the left of that road where it breasts the slope beyond the boundary is a field which is the probable location of Rupert's Bluecoats in their stubborn stand against Fairfax and D'Oyley. From the lay-by for the monument the view to the east is of Cromwell's horse's front line, and the gently mounded hill two fields over is Lodge Hill, the former rabbit warren. The view west from here, towards the monument, gives an impression of the hill the attacking Royalists had to climb before coming to blows with their adversaries on the summit of Closter ridge to the south.

Travelling farther north towards the Kelmarsh to Sibbertoft road takes the visitor along the line of the fighting retreat. Opposite the road junction at the end of this single-track road a public footpath runs on to the north to meet the Sibbertoft to Clipston road. The same point can be reached by car by turning left and then right at each of the next two road junctions. Looking northwards from the roadside opposite the footpath gives a view of the lines of retreat. Some fled down through the woods on the left, others ran to the right, back towards the flag on Moot Hill, where they made a stand. Continuing east from Sibbertoft, the road drops between the two lozenge-shaped fields of Nobold. The narrowness of the road and the height of the banks suggests how it could become jammed with fleeing people, forcing would-be escapers into the field to the north where they were caught and brutalized.

The next turning north is Dick's Hill, a single-track road which climbs between magnificent ridge-and-furrow on both sides. It is possible to park, with care, just before the road narrows and a little farther on, on the left, a stile gives access to a field in which the brick cube of a World War II Royal Observer Corps observation post stands. With footwear proof against sheep-droppings, the short walk to the Observer position gives superb views. From here Moot Hill and Wadborough can be seen and the

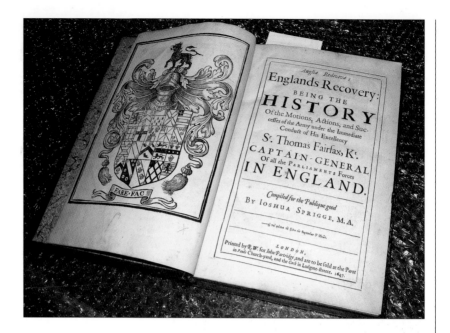

lines of flight in the valley either side of the wedge of woods that conceals a deep gully are evident. To the south the radio mast alongside the A14 can be seen and turning right from it Fairfax's original position, Naseby church spire, Mill Hill Farm, Longhold Spinney and Lowe Farm – the entire route of the Parliamentarian movement between 8am and about 3.00pm on 14 June 1645. To the north-east, depending on the time of year and thus the leaf-cover of the trees, East Farndon church and the Royalist line towards Little Oxendon can be identified – if not from the ROC post, then through a gateway on the road – and the Royalist lines of march become clear. It is a fitting climax to a tour of the battlefield.

The road from East Farndon to Market Harborough crosses a minor road at a mini-roundabout and runs alongside the western side of Welland Park before joining the A4304. Where this road passes over the bridge above the River Welland is the position of Bloodyman's Ford at which Charles was almost captured.

The Battlefields Trust resource centre on the website *www.battlefieldstrust.com/resource* gives detailed mapping and aerial photograph material useful to armchair and actual visitor alike and provides links to the latest information about the evolving provision of viewpoints and interpretation boards. The development of the visitor facilities by the Naseby Battlefield Project will continue for many years. The project's website *www.naseby.com* gives details of a self-guided tour and will be updated regularly as new facilities are completed. Supporters can also find forms for making donations to the funds.

BIBLIOGRAPHY

Art of Martiall Discipline, The, Perry Miniatures (2006)

Bagot, William, *Letters, 31–37*, James Marshall and Marie-Louise Osborn Collection, Beinecke Library, Yale University.

Barratt, John, *Cavaliers: The Royalist Army at War 1642–1646*, Sutton Publishing (2000)

Barriffe, William, ed. Keith Roberts, *Militarie Discipline: or the Young Artillery-man*, Gertrude Dawson (1661), reprinted Partizan Press (1988)

Blackmore, David, *Arms & Armour of the English Civil Wars*, Royal Armouries (1990)

_____,'Counting the New Model Army', *English Civil War Times No.58*, Leigh on Sea

Blackmore, Howard L., *British Military Firearms 1650–1850*, Herbert Jenkins (1961)

Clarendon, Edward Hyde, Earl of, ed. Roger Lockyer, *The History of the Great Rebellion*, Oxford University Press for The Folio Society (1967)

Courtney, Paul and Yolanda, 'A Siege Examined, the Civil War Archaeology of Leicester' in *Post-Medieval Archaeology* 26 (1992)

Cust, Richard, 'Why did Charles I Fight at Naseby?' in *History Today*, vol. 55 (10), October (2005)

Denton, Barry, *Naseby Fight*, Partizan Press (1988)

Ede-Borrett, Stephen, 'The Original Officer List of the New Model Army' in *Arquebusier*, vol. XXIX/III, Farnham (2006)

_____, 'Some Notes on the Raising and Origins of Colonel Okey's Regiment of Dragoons' in *The Journal of the Society for Army Historical Research* (forthcoming)

Edwards, Peter, 'Logistics and Supply' in Kenyon, John, and Jane Ohlmeyer, *The Civil Wars: A Military History of England, Scotland and Ireland 1638–1660*, Oxford University Press (1998)

Firth, Charles, *Cromwell's Army*, Methuen (1902)

Foard, Glenn, *Naseby: The Decisive Campaign*, Pryor Publications (1995)

Gardiner, S.R., *History of the Great Civil War*, vol. II, Longmans, Green (1889), Windrush Press (1987)

Gentles, Ian, *The New Model Army*, Blackwell (1992)

Grose, Francis, *Military Antiquities* vols I & II, 2nd edition, Stockdale (1812)

Gruber von Arni, Eric, *Justice to the Maimed Soldier*, Ashgate (2001)

Hughes, B.P., *Firepower: Weapons Effectiveness on the Battlefield 1630–1850*, Arms and Armour (1974)

Kitson, Frank, *Prince Rupert: Portrait of a Soldier*, Constable (1994)

Lockinge, Henry, *Historical Gleanings on the Memorable Field of Naseby*, Longman, Rees, Orme, Brown and Green (1830)

Marix Evans, Martin, Peter Burton and Michael Westaway, *Naseby*, Battleground Britain Series, Pen & Sword Books (2002)

Mastin, John, *The History and Antiquities of Naseby*, Francis Hodson (1792)

Newman, Peter R., *Companion to the English Civil Wars*, Facts on File (1990)

Peachey, Stuart, *The Mechanics of Infantry Combat in the First English Civil War*, Stuart Press (1992)

Phillips, John Roland, *Memoirs of the Civil War in Wales and the Marches*, vol. II, Longmans, Green (1874)

Reid, Stuart, *All the King's Armies*, Spellmount (1998)

_____, *Gunpowder Triumphant*, Partizan Press (no date)

Richards, Jeff, *The Siege and Storming of Leicester, May 1645*, New Millennium (2001)

Roberts, Keith, 'Battle Plans: The Practical Use of Battlefield Plans in the English Civil War' in *Cromwelliana*, The Cromwell Association (1997)

_____, *Cromwell's War Machine: The New Model Army 1645–1660*, Pen & Sword Books (2005)

_____, *Soldiers of the English Civil War 1: Infantry*, Elite Series, Osprey (1989)

Royal Commission on Historical Monuments, *An Inventory of the Historical Monuments in the County of Northampton*, vol. III, HMSO (1981)

Rupert, Prince Palatine, transcription Malcolm Wanklyn, *Diary*, Wiltshire CRO 413/444A

Singleton, Charles, *Composition of the Oxford Foot, Naseby 14 June 1645*, unpublished paper

Smith, Geoffrey Ridsdill and Margaret Toynbee, *Leaders of the Civil Wars 1642–1648*, The Roundwood Press (1977)

Symonds, Richard, ed. C.E. Long, *Diary of the Marches of the Royal Army*, Cambridge (1997)

Tennant, Philip, *Edgehill and Beyond: The People's War in the South Midlands 1642–1645*, Alan Sutton (1992)

Tibbutt, H.G., ed., *The Letter Books of Sir Samuel Luke*, HMSO (1963)

Tincey, John, *Ironsides: English Cavalry 1588–1688*, Warrior Series, Osprey (2002)

_____, *Soldiers of the English Civil War 2: Cavalry*, Elite Series, Osprey (1990)

Wanklyn, Malcolm, *Decisive Battles of the English Civil Wars: Myth and Reality*, Pen & Sword Books (2006)

_____ and Frank Jones, *A Military History of the English Civil War, 1642–1645*, Pearson Longman (2005)

Warburton, Eliot, *Memoirs of Prince Rupert and the Cavaliers*, Vol. III, Richard Bentley (1849)

Young, Peter, *Naseby 1645: The Campaign and the Battle*, Century (1985)

Note: The texts by those contemporary commentators or sources not listed above that are quoted in this work can be found in the appendix sections of Young or Foard.

INDEX

References to illustrations are shown in **bold**.

Abingdon 8, 10
Adwalton Moor, battle of (1643) 19
Anglia Rediviva 21, 29, **93** *see also* Sprigge,
    The Rev. Joshua
armies, opposing 22–33 *see also* New Model
    Army; Parliamentarian army; Royalist
    'Oxford' Army
    formations 22–24, 25, 26, 27
    tactics, fighting 24–27
armour **24**, 24, **28**
Art of Martiall Discipline, The **25**, **29**
Ashburnham, John 36
Ashby de la Zouch 11, 84
Astley, Lord (formerly Sir Jacob) 14, 16, 18, 31,
    34–35, 39, 43, 44, 90
Astley, Sir Bernard 43
Aylesbury 11

Bampton 38
Banbury 11
Bard, Col Sir Henry 31, 35, 39, 43, 44
Belasyse, John, Lord 18
Belvoir Castle 11
Bishop, George 71, 75
Blackmore, David 30
Blackmore, Howard 22
Blackiston, Sir William 35
Blechingdon 38
Boarstall House 46
Booth, Col George 42
Bourne, Maj Nehemiah 21
Brampton Bridge 11
Breitenfeld, first battle of (1631) 25
Brereton, Sir William 7–8, 15, 40–41
Bristol 7, 10, 11, 16, 17, 90
Britannia 14
Browne, Maj-Gen Richard 39
Burford 39
Butler, Col John 34, 66

Cambridge 10
campaign 38–48, 50–53
    Committee of Both Kingdoms responds
        39–41
    marches after fall of Leicester to 13 June **49**
    origins 7–14
        campaign of 1645 14
        centres of power 11–12
        logistical constraints 8–10
        military situation 7–8
        movement 13
    Oxford, the question of 41–42, 44–45
    Parliament responds: 2–13 June 45–48, 50
    Parliamentary preliminaries 38–39
    Royalists' opening moves 39
    Royalists' week: 7–13 June 50–53
    troop movements April to early June 1645 **40**
Campden House 39
Campion, Thomas 86
Carren, Nigel **9**, **24**, **28**, **31**
Cave, Sir Thomas 52
Charles I, King 7, 10, 15, 16, **17**, 17, **33**, 37, 39, **86**
    and battle of Naseby 54, 79

after battle 84, 90
captured correspondence **86**, 86
children **88**
execution **89**
letter to queen 44
strategy 36
Charles Louis, Prince of the Palatine **32**
Cheriton 26
Chester 8, 10, 11, 14, 15, 37, 40–41
chronology 15–16
Clarendon, Earl of (formerly Sir Edward Hyde)
    18, 78–79
Clark, Dr 86
Clubmen 10, 14
commanders, opposing 17–21
Committee of Both Kingdoms 7, 36, 37, 38,
    39–41, 46
Compton Winyates 39
Council of War 22
Cromwell, Oliver 14, 15, 19, **20**, 36, 38, 50, **90**
    at battle of Naseby 34, 56, 59, 61, 74, 79
    'Ironsides' 28, 39
Cropredy Bridge, battle of (1644) 7
Crowland 11
Culpepper, Sir John 41

Daventry 15, 45, 46, **50**, 50
    Borough Hill 15, 48, 51
de Gomme, Sir Bernard 26–27, **30**, 31
Digby, George, Lord 17, 36, 41, 44–45, 54,
    87–88, 89, 90
Doncaster 90
D'Oyley, Col Charles 75, 78
Dudley 10
Dunes, battle of the (1658) 26

East Anglia 8, 11
East Farndon 54, 55, 61, 91, 93
Eastern Association 28, 29, 30, 36, 37, 41
Edgehill, battle of (1642) 7, 17
Elton 26
equipment 22–23, 24 *see also* armour; gun-
    powder; munitions supplies; weapons
Essex, Earl of 7, 15, 28, 29, 30, 36
Evesham 39, 41

Fairfax, Sir Thomas **6**, 15, **19**, 19, 36, 38, 46, 47,
    48, **82**
    at Daventry 51
    and dragoons 29
    invests Oxford 39, 41
    at battle of Naseby 34, 56, 58, 75, 78, **82**
    after battle 90
Farmer, John 29
Faringdon castle 38
Fiennes, Col John 30, 34, 59, 61
Fitzgerald, Edward 84
foot, the 22–23, 29–30

Gerard, Charles 14, 31, 35
Gloucester 7, 10, 11
Goring, Lord 14, 15, 18, 19, 31, 37, 38, 39, 41,
    46, 54, 90
Greenwich 9
Grenville, Sir Richard 37

Grey, Col Henry 42
Guilsborough 15, 48, 50, 55
gunpowder 9, 23

Hammond, Col 34, 46, 71
Harrison, Maj Thomas 50
helmet, cheek piece **9**
helmet, trooper's three bar 'pot' **31**
Henrietta Maria, Queen 7, 17, 44
Hereford 90
Holborne, James 20
horse, the 23–24, 28
Howard, Thomas 32, 35, 87
Hull 9
Hyde, Sir Edward (later Earl of Clarendon) 18, 78–79

Innes, Maj James 42, 43
Ireland 7
Ireton, Col Henry 19, 34, 50, 59, 61, 66
Islip 15, 38

James I, King 6

King's Cabinet Opened, The **86**, 86
King's Lynn 9, 10
Kingdoms Weekly Intelligencer 75, 78
Kings Norton, Hawkesley Hall 39
Kislingbury 15, 48

Langdale, Sir Marmaduke 14, 15, 16, 18, 32, 39,
    53, **92**
    and battle of Naseby 35, 61, 71, 74, 79
Legge, Col William 37, 41, 44–45, 51, 87, 88–89
Leicester 11–12, 13, 15, 41, **42**, 42–44, **49**, 84, 90
Leven, Lord 36, 39–40, 90
Leverett, Capt John 21
Lindsey, Earl of 39
Lisle, Col George 18, 31, 35, 39, 43, 44, **82**
Little Oxendon 55
London, Tower of 8–9
Lostwithiel, battle of (1644) 7, 15, 17
Lubenham 52
Luke, Sir Oliver 40–41
Luke, Sir Samuel 21, 40–41, 46, 47, 48

Manchester, Earl of 7, 28, 29, 36
maps, contemporary **13**, **14**, **47**, **50**, **59**
Market Harborough 15, 52, 54, 83, 86, 93
Marston Moor, battle of (1644) 7, 15, 17, 19
Marston Trussell **83**, 84
Maurice, Prince 8, 14, 15, 18, 31, 37, 38, 39
    at battle of Naseby 34, **61**, 61, 62, 63
Militarie Discipline or the Young Artillery-man 24–25
Moderate Intelligencer, The 83–84
Montgomery, battle of (1644) 7–8
Monmouth 8
Montagu, Edward 20
Montrose, James Graham, Marquess of 15, 16,
    37, 40, 45
movement around the country 13
munitions supplies 9, **10**, 10 *see also* weapons

Naseby **52**, 53, 55, 59, **66**
    battlefield today **56**, **57**, **61**, **67**, **71**, **78**, **84**,
        91–93

monuments 91, **92**
Broadmoor 58, 63, **71**, **72–73**, 75
Closter Hill **67**, 67, 71, 75
Dick's Hill 83, **84**, 92–93
Dust Hill 56–58, 61, 62, **70**, **71**, 74, 75, 83, 91
Dust Hill Farm 91, **92**
'Englands' field **82**, **84**
Lodge Hill 58, **59**, 59, **71**, 71, 74, 92
Longhold Spinney **61**, **67**, 91, **92**, 93
Lowe Farm 91, 93
Mill Hill Farm 93
Moot Hill **78**, 78–79, **82**, **84**, 91, 92
Nobold Closes **76–77**, 92
Prince Rupert's Farm **61**, **75**, 91
Sibbertoft to Clipston road 78, 79, **82**, 92
Sulby Hedges **30**, 58, **61**, 61, 62, 66, **70**, **75**, 83, 90, 91–92
Sulby Hill 66
Wadborough Hill **76–77**, 79, **82**, 83, **84**, 91, 92
windmill 55
Naseby, battle of 15, **51**, 54–59, 61–63, **62**, 66–67, 71, 74–75, **75**, 78–79, 83–85
  battle area and troop movements before battle **60**
  battle begins 62–63, 66–67, 71
  battle plan **30**, 31, 54–55, **63**
  move to Dust Hill 56–58
  New Model Army advances 55–56
  orders of battle 34–35
  Royalist attack **64–65**
  Royalists' fighting retreat 75, 78–79, **82**
    second phase **71–72**
  Royalists' last stand **76–77**
    aftermath 86–90
    casualties 86
    final phase 79, 83–85
    fortunes of the king 90
    hindsight 87–90
  start of the day 54–55
  the battalia 58–59, 61–62
  the ground 58–59, 61–62, 67, 90
  turn of the tide 71, 74
New Model Army 15, 27–30 *see also*
  Parliamentarian army
  at battle of Naseby 55–56, 58–59, 61, 62, 66
  Butler's regiment 34, 66
  created 7, 9, 14, 19, 28
  Cromwell's regiments 28, 34, 39, 59, 71, 83, 92
  the dragoons 28–29
  Fairfax's Regiment 34, **82**
  Fiennes's Regiment 34, 59
  Forlorn Hope of Musketeers 34
  the foot 29–30
  Hammond's Regiment 34, 71
  the horse 28–29
  Ingoldsby's foot regiment 30, 38–39
  Ireton's regiments 30, 34, 38–39, 59, 66, 75
  marches away from Oxford 46
  Okey's Dragoons 21, 29, 34, **61**, 63, **70**, 83
  Pickering's Regiment 34, 67
  Pride's Regiment 34, 71
  Pye's Regiment 34, 59, 71, 74
  Rainsborough's Regiment 34, 71
  Rossiter's Regiment 34, 59, 61
  Skippon's regiments 34, 67, 71
  strength 30
  Vermuyden's Regiment 34, 66
  Waller's Regiment 34, 67
  Whalley's Regiment 34, 59, 71
Newark 11, 14, 41, 90
Newbury, battles of (1643) 7, 15
Newport Pagnell 11, 12, 30, **48**, 51
Nicholas, Sir Edward 36
Nichols, John 43, 44
North of England 7, 37, 45
Northampton 11, **13**, 13, 46, 47–48, **50**, 86

Northampton, Earl of 34, 38, 39, 43, 44, **70**, 87
Northamptonshire **47**, **50**
Northamptonshire Uplands 13
Norwich, Sir John 45, 46
Nottingham 11

Okey, Col John 21, 29, **30**, 34, **61**, 61–62, 63, 66, **70**, 83, 90
Oxford 7, 10, 11, 14, 15, 17, 36, 37, 38
  New College **8**
  siege of 15, 16, 39, 41–42, 44–45, 46, 90

Parliament controls South-East and East Anglia 8–9
Parliamentarian army 7 *see also* New Model Army
  Fortescue's regiment 38
  Graves's horse 38
  London Trained Bands 19–20
  preliminaries 38–39
Parliamentarian commanders 19–21
Parliamentarian plans 36
Parliamentarian response: 2–13 June 1645 45–48, 50
pikemen 23, 26, **29**
plans, opposing 36–37
Pontefract 14, 15
Portsmouth 9
Pride, Thomas 20, 34, 71
Purefoy, Maj George 39
Pye, Sir Robert 34, 42, 59, 71, 74

Radcot Bridge 38
Raglan Castle 90
Rainsborough, Col Thomas 6, 21, 34, 71
Rainsborough, Capt William 21
Reading 9, 10, 15, 38
Reid, Stuart 32
Richmond, Duke of 36, 39
Rockingham 11, 86
Rockingham Castle 45
Royalist commanders 17–19
Royalist 'Oxford' Army 7, 15, 30–33
  Astley's tertia 31, 34–35, 39, 43, 44
  Bard's tertia 31, 35, 39, 43, 44
  at battle of Naseby 61, 63, 66, 67, **70**, 71, **72–73**, 74
    attack **64–65**
    fighting retreat **72–73**, 75, 78–79
    last stand **76–77**
  campaign, opening moves in 39
  campaign, week of 7–13 June 1645 50–53
  Duke of York's Regiment of Foot 35, 66
  Gerard's battalion 31, 35
  Howard's battalion 35, 87
  King's Lifeguard 31, 32, 35, 39, 44, 74, **82**
  Langdale's divisions 32, 35, 39, 53, 61, 71, 74, 79, **92**
  Lisle's tertia 31, 35, 39, 43, 44, **82**
  Lundsford's Regiment 39
  Newark Horse 32, 35
  Northampton's Regiment of Horse 34, 43, 44, **70**, 87
  Northern Horse 14, 35, 71, 74, 75
  Prince Maurice's horse 34, **61**, 61, 62
  Prince Rupert's Bluecoats 31–32, 33, 34, 39, 43, 44, 74, **75**, 75, **92**, 92
  Queen's Regiment of Horse 34, **70**
  St George's Regiment 31, 35
  'Shrewsbury Foot' (Irish regiments) 8, 31, 33, 35, 43, 78
    strength 31–33
  Thomas's battalion 31
Royalist plans 37
Ruce, Francis 56–57
Rupert, Prince 11–12, 15, 16, 17, **32**, 39, 87, 90

and battle of Naseby 34, 54, 57, 63, 66, 74, 79
Bluecoats 31–32, 33, 34, 39, 43, 44, 74, **75**, 75, **92**, 92
in Daventry 50–51
as king's adviser 36
becomes Lord General 8
1645 campaign 14
in South Wales and the Marches 37
taking of Leicester 43
Rushworth, Frances/John 21, 62, 66, 79, **82**, 86

St George, Col William 31, 35, 43
Salisbury 14
Saxton, Christopher 13
Scots 7, 15, 36, 39–40, 41, 44, 90
Sherington 46
Shrewsbury 8, 15
Sibbertoft 58, 78
Skippon, Sgt-Maj-Gen Philip 11, 19–20, 34, 46, 56, 59, **66**, 67, 71, 86, 90
Slingsby, Sir Henry 18, 39, 42, 43, 52, 53, 56, 57, 62, 63, 74, 83
Slingsby, Col Walter 26
South-East England 8–9
Sprigge, The Rev. Joshua 21, 29, 46, 48, 86, **93**
  and battle of Naseby 55, 56, 59, 66, 67, 74, 75, 79
Stanford on Avon 52
Stony Stratford 15, 47
Stoughton, Lt-Col Israel 21
Stourbridge 10
Stow-on-the-Wold 16, 37, 39, 90
supplies 9, 10, 11
Symmons, Edward 86–87
Symonds, Richard 19, 32, 38, 39, 43, 44, 45, 50, 51, 54, 90

tactics, fighting 24–27
Taunton, siege of 14, 15, 30, 36, 37, 38, 39, 54
territory controlled in early 1645 **12**
Thames, River 10
Theddingworth 52–53
Tillier, Maj Henry 26
Towcester 7, 11, 15, 51
towns controlled in early 1645 **12**
True Informer, The 11
Turner, Sir James 22, 25

Vaughan, Col Sir William 38, 66, 90
Vermuyden, Col Bartholomew 15, 34, 41, 46, 47, 66
Vernon, John 23–24, 27
Vindication of King Charles, A **86**, 87

Walker, Sir Edward 18, 34, 36, 39, 41, 45, 51–52
  and battle of Naseby 54–55, 57, 67, 74, 75, 79
Waller, Sir Hardress 20
Waller, Sir William 7, 14, 29, 30, 36, 67
Wallingford 10
Watson, Maj Leonard 50
weapons 22–23, 24, 26 *see also* munitions
  musket exercises **25**
Weldon, Col 38
Welsh Marches 14, 37
West Country 7
Weymouth 8
Whetham, Maj (later Col) Nathaniel 11, 21, 46, 50, 52
Whitbroke, Lt-Col 42
Whitelocke, Bulstrode 21, 75
Willys, Sir Richard 45
Winter, Gen Daniel 86
Wogan, Capt Edward 21, 89
Woolwich Arsenal 8–9

York, Duke of 26, 31, 35, 66
Young Horseman, The 23–24